The Valley of Si

A Story of the Three River Country

James Oliver Curwood

Alpha Editions

This edition published in 2024

ISBN : 9789362095770

Design and Setting By
Alpha Editions
www.alphaedis.com
Email - info@alphaedis.com

Contents

THE VALLEY OF SILENT MEN

Before the railroad's thin lines of steel bit their way up through the wilderness, Athabasca Landing was the picturesque threshold over which one must step who would enter into the mystery and adventure of the great white North. It is still *Iskwatam*—the "door" which opens to the lower reaches of the Athabasca, the Slave, and the Mackenzie. It is somewhat difficult to find on the map, yet it is there, because its history is written in more than a hundred and forty years of romance and tragedy and adventure in the lives of men, and is not easily forgotten. Over the old trail it was about a hundred and fifty miles north of Edmonton. The railroad has brought it nearer to that base of civilization, but beyond it the wilderness still howls as it has howled for a thousand years, and the waters of a continent flow north and into the Arctic Ocean. It is possible that the beautiful dream of the real-estate dealers may come true, for the most avid of all the sportsmen of the earth, the money-hunters, have come up on the bumpy railroad that sometimes lights its sleeping cars with lanterns, and with them have come typewriters, and stenographers, and the art of printing advertisements, and the Golden Rule of those who sell handfuls of earth to hopeful purchasers thousands of miles away—"Do others as they would do you." And with it, too, has come the legitimate business of barter and trade, with eyes on all that treasure of the North which lies between the Grand Rapids of the Athabasca and the edge of the polar sea. But still more beautiful than the dream of fortunes quickly made is the deep-forest superstition that the spirits of the wilderness dead move onward as steam and steel advance, and if this is so, the ghosts of a thousand Pierres and Jacquelines have risen uneasily from their graves at Athabasca Landing, hunting a new quiet farther north.

For it was Pierre and Jacqueline, Henri and Marie, Jacques and his Jeanne, whose brown hands for a hundred and forty years opened and closed this door. And those hands still master a savage world for two thousand miles north of that threshold of Athabasca Landing. South of it a wheezy engine drags up the freight that came not so many months ago by boat.

It is over this threshold that the dark eyes of Pierre and Jacqueline, Henri and Marie, Jacques and his Jeanne, look into the blue and the gray and the sometimes watery ones of a destroying civilization. And there it is that the shriek of a mad locomotive mingles with their age-old river chants; the smut of coal drifts over their forests; the phonograph screeches its reply to *le violon*; and Pierre and Henri and Jacques no longer find themselves the kings of the earth when they come in from far countries with their precious cargoes of furs. And they no longer swagger and tell loud-voiced adventure, or sing their wild river songs in the same old abandon, for there are streets at Athabasca Landing now, and hotels, and schools, and rules and regulations of a kind new and terrifying to the bold of the old *voyageurs*.

It seems only yesterday that the railroad was not there, and a great world of wilderness lay between the Landing and the upper rim of civilization. And when word first came that a steam thing was eating its way up foot by foot through forest and swamp and impassable muskeg, that word passed up and down the water-ways for two thousand miles, a colossal joke, a stupendous bit of drollery, the funniest thing that Pierre and Henri and Jacques had heard in all their lives. And when Jacques wanted to impress upon Pierre his utter disbelief of a thing, he would say:

"It will happen, m'sieu, when the steam thing comes to the Landing, when cow-beasts eat with the moose, and when our bread is found for us in yonder swamps!"

And the steam thing came, and cows grazed where moose had fed, and bread WAS gathered close to the edge of the great swamps. Thus did civilization break into Athabasca Landing.

Northward from the Landing, for two thousand miles, reached the domain of the rivermen. And the Landing, with its two hundred and twenty-seven souls before the railroad came, was the wilderness clearing-house which sat at the beginning of things. To it came from the south all the freight which must go into the north; on its flat river front were built the great scows which carried this freight to the end of the earth. It was from the Landing that the greatest of all river brigades set forth upon their long adventures, and it was back to the Landing, perhaps a year or more later, that still smaller scows and huge canoes brought as the price of exchange their cargoes of furs.

Thus for nearly a century and a half the larger craft, with their great sweeps and their wild-throated crews, had gone *down* the river toward the Arctic Ocean, and the smaller craft, with their still wilder crews, had come *up* the river toward civilization. The River, as the Landing speaks of it, is the Athabasca, with its headwaters away off in the British Columbian mountains, where Baptiste and McLeod, explorers of old, gave up their lives to find where the cradle of it lay. And it sweeps past the Landing, a slow and mighty giant, unswervingly on its way to the northern sea. With it the river brigades set forth. For Pierre and Henri and Jacques it is going from one end to the other of the earth. The Athabasca ends and is replaced by the Slave, and the Slave empties into Great Slave Lake, and from the narrow tip of that Lake the Mackenzie carries on for more than a thousand miles to the sea.

In this distance of the long water trail one sees and hears many things. It is life. It is adventure. It is mystery and romance and hazard. Its tales are so many that books could not hold them. In the faces of men and women they are written. They lie buried in graves so old that the forest trees grow over them. Epics of tragedy, of love, of the fight to live! And as one goes farther north, and still farther, just so do the stories of things that have happened change.

For the world is changing, the sun is changing, and the breeds of men are changing. At the Landing in July there are seventeen hours of sunlight; at Fort Chippewyan there are eighteen; at Fort Resolution, Fort Simpson, and Fort Providence there are nineteen; at the Great Bear twenty-one, and at Fort McPherson, close to the polar sea, from twenty-two to twenty-three. And in December there are also these hours of darkness. With light and darkness men change, women change, and life changes. And Pierre and Henri and Jacques meet them all, but always THEY are the same, chanting the old songs, enshrining the old loves, dreaming the same dreams, and worshiping always the same gods. They meet a thousand perils with eyes that glisten with the love of adventure.

The thunder of rapids and the howlings of storm do not frighten them. Death has no fear for them. They grapple with it, wrestle joyously with it, and are glorious when they win. Their blood is red and strong. Their hearts are big. Their souls chant themselves up to the skies. Yet they are simple as children, and when they are afraid, it is of things which children fear. For in those hearts of theirs is superstition—and also, perhaps, royal blood. For princes and the sons of princes and the noblest aristocracy of France were the first of the gentlemen adventurers who came with ruffles on their sleeves and rapiers at their sides to seek furs worth many times their weight in gold two hundred and fifty years ago, and of these ancient forebears Pierre and Henri and Jacques, with their Maries and Jeannes and Jacquelines, are the living voices of today.

And these voices tell many stories. Sometimes they whisper them, as the wind would whisper, for there are stories weird and strange that must be spoken softly. They darken no printed pages. The trees listen to them beside red camp-fires at night. Lovers tell them in the glad sunshine of day. Some of them are chanted in song. Some of them come down through the generations, epics of the wilderness, remembered from father to son. And each year there are the new things to pass from mouth to mouth, from cabin to cabin, from the lower reaches of the Mackenzie to the far end of the world at Athabasca Landing. For the three rivers are always makers of romance, of tragedy, of adventure. The story will never be forgotten of how Follette and Ladouceur swam their mad race through the Death Chute for love of the girl who waited at the other end, or of how Campbell O'Doone, the red-headed giant at Fort Resolution, fought the whole of a great brigade in his effort to run away with a scow captain's daughter.

And the brigade loved O'Doone, though it beat him, for these men of the strong north love courage and daring. The epic of the lost scow—how there were men who saw it disappear from under their very eyes, floating upward and afterward riding swiftly away in the skies—is told and retold by strong-faced men, deep in whose eyes are the smoldering flames of an undying superstition, and these same men thrill as they tell over again the strange and unbelievable story of Hartshope, the aristocratic Englishman who set off into the North in all the glory of monocle and unprecedented luggage, and how he joined in a tribal war, became a chief of the Dog Ribs, and married a dark-eyed, sleek-haired, little Indian beauty, who is now the mother of his children.

But deepest and most thrilling of all the stories they tell are the stories of the long arm of the Law—that arm which reaches for two thousand miles from Athabasca Landing to the polar sea, the arm Of the Royal Northwest Mounted Police.

And of these it is the story of Jim Kent we are going to tell, of Jim Kent and of Marette, that wonderful little goddess of the Valley of Silent Men, in whose veins there must have run the blood of fighting men—and of ancient queens. A story of the days before the railroad came.

CHAPTER I

In the mind of James Grenfell Kent, sergeant in the Royal Northwest Mounted Police, there remained no shadow of a doubt. He knew that he was dying. He had implicit faith in Cardigan, his surgeon friend, and Cardigan had told him that what was left of his life would be measured out in hours— perhaps in minutes or seconds. It was an unusual case. There was one chance in fifty that he might live two or three days, but there was no chance at all that he would live more than three. The end might come with any breath he drew into his lungs. That was the pathological history of the thing, as far as medical and surgical science knew of cases similar to his own.

Personally, Kent did not feel like a dying man. His vision and his brain were clear. He felt no pain, and only at infrequent intervals was his temperature above normal. His voice was particularly calm and natural.

At first he had smiled incredulously when Cardigan broke the news. That the bullet which a drunken half-breed had sent into his chest two weeks before had nicked the arch of the aorta, thus forming an aneurism, was a statement by Cardigan which did not sound especially wicked or convincing to him. "Aorta" and "aneurism" held about as much significance for him as his perichondrium or the process of his stylomastoid. But Kent possessed an unswerving passion to grip at facts in detail, a characteristic that had largely helped him to earn the reputation of being the best man-hunter in all the northland service. So he had insisted, and his surgeon friend had explained.

The aorta, he found, was the main blood-vessel arching over and leading from the heart, and in nicking it the bullet had so weakened its outer wall that it bulged out in the form of a sack, just as the inner tube of an automobile tire bulges through the outer casing when there is a blowout.

"And when that sack gives way inside you," Cardigan had explained, "you'll go like that!" He snapped a forefinger and thumb to drive the fact home.

After that it was merely a matter of common sense to believe, and now, sure that he was about to die. Kent had acted. He was acting in the full health of his mind and in extreme cognizance of the paralyzing shock he was contributing as a final legacy to the world at large, or at least to that part of it which knew him or was interested. The tragedy of the thing did not oppress him. A thousand times in his life he had discovered that humor and tragedy were very closely related, and that there were times when only the breadth of a hair separated the two. Many times he had seen a laugh change suddenly to tears, and tears to laughter.

The tableau, as it presented itself about his bedside now, amused him. Its humor was grim, but even in these last hours of his life he appreciated it. He had always more or less regarded life as a joke—a very serious joke, but a joke for all that—a whimsical and trickful sort of thing played by the Great Arbiter on humanity at large; and this last count in his own life, as it was solemnly and tragically ticking itself off, was the greatest joke of all. The amazed faces that stared at him, their passing moments of disbelief, their repressed but at times visible betrayals of horror, the steadiness of their eyes, the tenseness of their lips—all added to what he might have called, at another time, the dramatic artistry of his last great adventure.

That he was dying did not chill him, or make him afraid, or put a tremble into his voice. The contemplation of throwing off the mere habit of breathing had never at any stage of his thirty-six years of life appalled him. Those years, because he had spent a sufficient number of them in the raw places of the earth, had given him a philosophy and viewpoint of his own, both of which he kept unto himself without effort to impress them on other people. He believed that life itself was the cheapest thing on the face of all the earth. All other things had their limitations.

There was so much water and so much land, so many mountains and so many plains, so many square feet to live on and so many square feet to be buried in. All things could be measured, and stood up, and catalogued—except life itself. "Given time," he would say, "a single pair of humans can populate all creation." Therefore, being the cheapest of all things, it was true philosophy that life should be the easiest of all things to give up when the necessity came.

Which is only another way of emphasizing that Kent was not, and never had been, afraid to die. But it does not say that he treasured life a whit less than the man in another room, who, a day or so before, had fought like a lunatic before going under an anesthetic for the amputation of a bad finger. No man had loved life more than he. No man had lived nearer it.

It had been a passion with him. Full of dreams, and always with anticipations ahead, no matter how far short realizations fell, he was an optimist, a lover of the sun and the moon and the stars, a worshiper of the forests and of the mountains, a man who loved his life, and who had fought for it, and yet who was ready—at the last—to yield it up without a whimper when the fates asked for it.

Bolstered up against his pillows, he did not look the part of the fiend he was confessing himself to be to the people about him. Sickness had not emaciated him. The bronze of his lean, clean-cut face had faded a little, but the tanning of wind and sun and campfire was still there. His blue eyes were perhaps dulled somewhat by the nearness of death. One would not have judged him to be thirty-six, even though over one temple there was a streak of gray in his blond hair—a heritage from his mother, who was dead. Looking at him, as his lips quietly and calmly confessed himself beyond the pale of men's sympathy or forgiveness, one would have said that his crime was impossible.

Through his window, as he sat bolstered up in his cot, Kent could see the slow-moving shimmer of the great Athabasca River as it moved on its way toward the Arctic Ocean. The sun was shining, and he saw the cool, thick masses of the spruce and cedar forests beyond, the rising undulations of wilderness ridges and hills, and through that open window he caught the sweet scents that came with a soft wind from out of the forests he had loved for so many years.

"They've been my best friends," he had said to Cardigan, "and when this nice little thing you're promising happens to me, old man, I want to go with my eyes on them."

So his cot was close to the window.

Nearest to him sat Cardigan. In his face, more than in any of the others, was disbelief. Kedsty, Inspector of the Royal Northwest Mounted Police, in charge of N Division during an indefinite leave of absence of the superintendent, was paler even than the girl whose nervous fingers were swiftly putting upon paper every word that was spoken by those in the room. O'Connor, staff-sergeant, was like one struck dumb. The little, smooth-faced Catholic missioner whose presence as a witness Kent had requested, sat with his thin fingers tightly interlaced, silently placing this among all the other strange tragedies that the wilderness had given up to him. They had all been Kent's friends, his intimate friends, with the exception of the girl, whom Inspector Kedsty had borrowed for the occasion. With the little missioner he had spent many an evening, exchanging in mutual confidence the strange and mysterious happenings of the deep forests, and of the great north beyond the forests. O'Connor's friendship was a friendship bred of the brotherhood of the trails. It was Kent and O'Connor who had brought down the two Eskimo murderers from the mouth of the Mackenzie, and the adventure had taken them fourteen months. Kent loved O'Connor, with his red face, his red hair, and his big heart, and to him the most tragic part of it all was that he was breaking this friendship now.

But it was Inspector Kedsty, commanding N Division, the biggest and wildest division in all the Northland, that roused in Kent an unusual emotion, even as he waited for that explosion just over his heart which the surgeon had told him might occur at any moment. On his death-bed his mind still worked analytically. And Kedsty, since the moment he had entered the room, had puzzled Kent. The commander of N Division was an unusual man. He was sixty, with iron-gray hair, cold, almost colorless eyes in which one would search long for a gleam of either mercy or fear, and a nerve that Kent had never seen even slightly disturbed. It took such a man, an iron man, to run

N Division according to law, for N Division covered an area of six hundred and twenty thousand square miles of wildest North America, extending more than two thousand miles north of the 70th parallel of latitude, with its farthest limit three and one-half degrees within the Arctic Circle. To police this area meant upholding the law in a country fourteen times the size of the state of Ohio. And Kedsty was the man who had performed this duty as only one other man had ever succeeded in doing it.

Yet Kedsty, of the five about Kent, was most disturbed. His face was ash-gray. A number of times Kent had detected a broken note in his voice. He had seen his hands grip at the arms of the chair he sat in until the cords stood out on them as if about to burst. He had never seen Kedsty sweat until now.

Twice the Inspector had wiped his forehead with a handkerchief. He was no longer *Minisak*—"The Rock"—a name given to him by the Crees. The armor that no shaft had ever penetrated seemed to have dropped from him. He had ceased to be Kedsty, the most dreaded inquisitor in the service. He was nervous, and Kent could see that he was fighting to repossess himself.

"Of course you know what this means to the Service," he said in a hard, low voice. "It means—"

"Disgrace," nodded Kent. "I know. It means a black spot on the otherwise bright escutcheon of N Division. But it can't be helped. I killed John Barkley. The man you've got in the guard-house, condemned to be hanged by the neck until he is dead, is innocent. I understand. It won't be nice for the Service to let it be known that a sergeant in His Majesty's Royal Mounted is an ordinary murderer, but—"

"Not an *ordinary* murderer," interrupted Kedsty. "As you have described it, the crime was deliberate—horrible and inexcusable to its last detail. You were not moved by a sudden passion. You tortured your victim. It is inconceivable!"

"And yet true," said Kent.

He was looking at the stenographer's slim fingers as they put down his words and Kedsty's. A bit of sunshine touched her bowed head, and he observed the red lights in her hair. His eyes swept to O'Connor, and in that moment the commander of N Division bent over him, so close that his face almost touched Kent's, and he whispered, in a voice so low that no one of the other four could hear,

"*Kent—you lie!*"

"No, it is true," replied Kent.

Kedsty drew back, again wiping the moisture from his forehead.

"I killed Barkley, and I killed him as I planned that he should die," Kent went on. "It was my desire that he should suffer. The one thing which I shall not tell you is *why* I killed him. But it was a sufficient reason."

He saw the shuddering tremor that swept through the shoulders of the girl who was putting down the condemning notes.

"And you refuse to confess your motive?"

"Absolutely—except that he had wronged me in a way that deserved death."

"And you make this confession knowing that you are about to die?"

The flicker of a smile passed over Kent's lips. He looked at O'Connor and for an instant saw in O'Connor's eyes a flash of their old comradeship.

"Yes. Dr. Cardigan has told me. Otherwise I should have let the man in the guard-house hang. It's simply that this accursed bullet has spoiled my luck—and saved him!"

Kedsty spoke to the girl. For half an hour she read her notes, and after that Kent wrote his name on the last page. Then Kedsty rose from his chair.

"We have finished, gentlemen," he said.

They trailed out, the girl hurrying through the door first in her desire to free herself of an ordeal that had strained every nerve in her body. The commander of N Division was last to go. Cardigan hesitated, as if to remain, but Kedsty motioned him on. It was Kedsty who closed the door, and as he closed it he looked back, and for a flash Kent met his eyes squarely. In that moment he received an impression which he had not caught while the Inspector was in the room. It was like an electrical shock in its unexpectedness, and Kedsty must have seen the effect of it in his face, for he moved back quickly and closed the door. In that instant Kent had seen in Kedsty's eyes and face a look that was not only of horror, but what in the face and eyes of another man he would have sworn was fear.

It was a gruesome moment in which to smile, but Kent smiled. The shock was over. By the rules of the Criminal Code he knew that Kedsty even now was instructing Staff-Sergeant O'Connor to detail an officer to guard his door. The fact that he was ready to pop off at any moment would make no difference in the regulations of the law. And Kedsty was a stickler for the law as it was written. Through the closed door he heard voices indistinctly. Then there were footsteps, dying away. He could hear the heavy thump, thump of O'Connor's big feet. O'Connor had always walked like that, even on the trail.

Softly then the door reopened, and Father Layonne, the little missioner, came in. Kent knew that this would be so, for Father Layonne knew neither code nor creed that did not reach all the hearts of the wilderness. He came back, and sat down close to Kent, and took one of his hands and held it closely in both of his own. They were not the soft, smooth hands of the priestly hierarchy, but were hard with the callosity of toil, yet gentle with the gentleness of a great sympathy. He had loved Kent yesterday, when Kent had stood clean in the eyes of both God and men, and he still loved him today, when his soul was stained with a thing that must be washed away with his own life.

"I'm sorry, lad," he said. "I'm sorry."

Something rose up in Kent's throat that was not the blood he had been wiping away since morning. His fingers returned the pressure of the little missioner's hands. Then he pointed out through the window to the panorama of shimmering river and green forests.

"It is hard to say good-by to all that, Father," he said. "But, if you don't mind, I'd rather not talk about it. I'm not afraid of it. And why be unhappy because one has only a little while to live? Looking back over your life, does it seem so very long ago that you were a boy, a small boy?"

"The time has gone swiftly, very swiftly."

"It seems only yesterday—or so?"

"Yes, only yesterday—or so."

Kent's face lit up with the whimsical smile that long ago had reached the little missioner's heart. "Well, that's the way I'm looking at it, Father. There is only a yesterday, a today, and a tomorrow in the longest of our lives. Looking back from seventy years isn't much different from looking back from thirty-six *when* you're looking back and not ahead. Do you think what I have just said will free Sandy McTrigger?"

"There is no doubt. Your statements have been accepted as a death-bed confession."

The little missioner, instead of Kent, was betraying a bit of nervousness.

"There are matters, my son—some few matters—which you will want attended to. Shall we not talk about them?"

"You mean—"

"Your people, first. I remember that once you told me there was no one. But surely there is some one somewhere."

Kent shook his head. "There is no one now. For ten years those forests out there have been father, mother, and home to me."

"But there must be personal affairs, affairs which you would like to entrust, perhaps, to me?"

Kent's face brightened, and for an instant a flash of humor leaped into his eyes. "It is funny," he chuckled. "Since you remind me of it, Father, it is quite in form to make my will. I've bought a few little pieces of land here. Now that the railroad has almost reached us from Edmonton, they've jumped up from the seven or eight hundred dollars I gave for them to about ten thousand. I want you to sell the lots and use the money in your work. Put as much of it on the Indians as you can. They've always been good brothers to me. And I wouldn't waste much time in getting my signature on some sort of paper to that effect."

Father Layonne's eyes shone softly. "God will bless you for that, Jimmy," he said, using the intimate name by which he had known him. "And I think He is going to pardon you for something else, if you have the courage to ask Him."

"I am pardoned," replied Kent, looking out through the window. "I feel it. I know it, Father."

In his soul the little missioner was praying. He knew that Kent's religion was not his religion, and he did not press the service which he would otherwise have rendered. After a moment he rose to his feet, and it was the old Kent who looked up into his face, the clean-faced, gray-eyed, unafraid Kent, smiling in the old way.

"I have one big favor to ask of you, Father," he said. "If I've got a day to live, I don't want every one forcing the fact on me that I'm dying. If I've any friends left, I want them to come in and see me, and talk, and crack jokes. I want to smoke my pipe. I'll appreciate a box of cigars if you'll send 'em up. Cardigan can't object now. Will you arrange these things for me? They'll listen to you—and please shove my cot a little nearer the window before you go."

Father Layonne performed the service in silence. Then at last the yearning overcame him to have the soul speak out, that his God might be more merciful, and he said: "My boy, you are sorry? You repent that you killed John Barkley?"

"No, I'm not sorry. It had to be done. And please don't forget the cigars, will you, Father?"

"No, I won't forget," said the little missioner, and turned away.

As the door opened and closed behind him, the flash of humor leaped into Kent's eyes again, and he chuckled even as he wiped another of the telltale stains of blood from his lips. He had played the game. And the funny part

about it was that no one in all the world would ever know, except himself—
and perhaps one other.

CHAPTER II

Outside Kent's window was Spring, the glorious Spring of the Northland, and in spite of the death-grip that was tightening in his chest he drank it in deeply and leaned over so that his eyes traveled over wide spaces of the world that had been his only a short time before.

It occurred to him that he had suggested this knoll that overlooked both settlement and river as the site for the building which Dr. Cardigan called his hospital. It was a structure rough and unadorned, unpainted, and sweetly smelling with the aroma of the spruce trees from the heart of which its unplaned lumber was cut. The breath of it was a thing to bring cheer and hope. Its silvery walls, in places golden and brown with pitch and freckled with knots, spoke joyously of life that would not die, and the woodpeckers came and hammered on it as though it were still a part of the forest, and red squirrels chattered on the roof and scampered about in play with a soft patter of feet.

"It's a pretty poor specimen of man that would die up here with all that under his eyes," Kent had said a year before, when he and Cardigan had picked out the site. "If he died looking at that, why, he just simply ought to die, Cardigan," he had laughed.

And now he was that poor specimen, looking out on the glory of the world!

His vision took in the South and a part of the East and West, and in all those directions there was no end of the forest. It was like a vast, many-colored sea with uneven billows rising and falling until the blue sky came down to meet them many miles away. More than once his heart ached at the thought of the two thin ribs of steel creeping up foot by foot and mile by mile from Edmonton, a hundred and fifty miles away. It was, to him, a desecration, a crime against Nature, the murder of his beloved wilderness. For in his soul that wilderness had grown to be more than a thing of spruce and cedar and balsam, of poplar and birch; more than a great, unused world of river and lake and swamp. It was an individual, a thing. His love for it was greater than his love for man. It was his inarticulate God. It held him as no religion in the world could have held him, and deeper and deeper it had drawn him into the soul of itself, delivering up to him one by one its guarded secrets and its mysteries, opening for him page by page the book that was the greatest of all books. And it was the wonder of it now, the fact that it was near him, about him, embracing him, glowing for him in the sunshine, whispering to him in the soft breath of the air, nodding and talking to him from the crest of every ridge, that gave to him a strange happiness even in these hours when he knew that he was dying.

And then his eyes fell nearer to the settlement which nestled along the edge of the shining river a quarter of a mile away. That, too, had been the wilderness, in the days before the railroad came. The poison of speculation was stirring, but it had not yet destroyed. Athabasca Landing was still the door that opened and closed on the great North. Its buildings were scattered and few, and built of logs and rough lumber. Even now he could hear the drowsy hum of the distant sawmill that was lazily turning out its grist. Not far away the wind-worn flag of the British Empire was floating over a Hudson Bay Company's post that had bartered in the trades of the North for more than a hundred years. Through that hundred years Athabasca Landing had pulsed with the heart-beats of strong men bred to the wilderness. Through it, working its way by river and dog sledge from the South, had gone the precious freight for which the farther North gave in exchange its still more precious furs. And today, as Kent looked down upon it, he saw that same activity as it had existed through the years of a century. A brigade of scows, laden to their gunwales, was just sweeping out into the river and into its current. Kent had watched the loading of them; now he saw them drifting lazily out from the shore, their long sweeps glinting in the sun, their crews singing wildly and fiercely their beloved Chanson des Voyageurs as their faces turned to the adventure of the North.

In Kent's throat rose a thing which he tried to choke back, but which broke from his lips in a low cry, almost a sob. He heard the distant singing, wild and free as the forests themselves, and he wanted to lean out of his window and shout a last good-by. For the brigade—a Company brigade, the brigade that had chanted its songs up and down the water reaches of the land for more than two hundred and fifty years—was starting north. And he knew where it was going—north, and still farther north; a hundred miles, five hundred, a thousand—and then another thousand before the last of the scows unburdened itself of its precious freight. For the lean and brown-visaged men who went with them there would be many months of clean living and joyous thrill under the open skies. Overwhelmed by the yearning that swept over him, Kent leaned back against his pillows and covered his eyes.

In those moments his brain painted for him swiftly and vividly the things he was losing. Tomorrow or next day he would be dead, and the river brigade would still be sweeping on—on into the Grand Rapids of the Athabasca, fighting the Death Chute, hazarding valiantly the rocks and rapids of the Grand Cascade, the whirlpools of the Devil's Mouth, the thundering roar and boiling dragon teeth of the Black Run—on to the end of the Athabasca, to the Slave, and into the Mackenzie, until the last rock-blunted nose of the outfit drank the tide-water of the Arctic Ocean. And he, James Kent, would be DEAD!

He uncovered his eyes, and there was a wan smile on his lips as he looked forth once more. There were sixteen scows in the brigade, and the biggest, he knew, was captained by Pierre Rossand. He could fancy Pierre's big red throat swelling in mighty song, for Pierre's wife was waiting for him a thousand miles away. The scows were caught steadily now in the grip of the river, and it seemed to Kent, as he watched them go, that they were the last fugitives fleeing from the encroaching monsters of steel. Unconscious of the act, he reached out his arms, and his soul cried out its farewell, even though his lips were silent.

He was glad when they were gone and when the voices of the chanting oarsmen were lost in the distance. Again he listened to the lazy hum of the sawmill, and over his head he heard the velvety run of a red squirrel and then its reckless chattering. The forests came back to him. Across his cot fell a patch of golden sunlight. A stronger breath of air came laden with the perfume of balsam and cedar through his window, and when the door opened and Cardigan entered, he found the old Kent facing him.

There was no change in Cardigan's voice or manner as he greeted him. But there was a tenseness in his face which he could not conceal. He had brought in Kent's pipe and tobacco. These he laid on a table until he had placed his head close to Kent's hearty listening to what he called the *bruit*—the rushing of blood through the aneurismal sac.

"Seems to me that I can hear it myself now and then," said Kent. "Worse, isn't it?"

Cardigan nodded. "Smoking may hurry it up a bit," he said. "Still, if you want to—"

Kent held out his hand for the pipe and tobacco. "It's worth it. Thanks, old man."

Kent loaded the pipe, and Cardigan lighted a match. For the first time in two weeks a cloud of smoke issued from between Kent's lips.

"The brigade is starting north," he said.

"Mostly Mackenzie River freight," replied Cardigan. "A long run."

"The finest in all the North. Three years ago O'Connor and I made it with the Follette outfit. Remember Follette—and Ladouceur? They both loved the same girl, and being good friends they decided to settle the matter by a swim through the Death Chute. The man who came through first was to have her. Gawd, Cardigan, what funny things happen! Follette came out first, but he was dead. He'd brained himself on a rock. And to this day Ladouceur hasn't married the girl, because he says Follette beat him; and that Follette's something-or-other would haunt him if he didn't play fair. It's a queer—"

He stopped and listened. In the hall was the approaching tread of unmistakable feet.

"O'Connor," he said.

Cardigan went to the door and opened it as O'Connor was about to knock. When the door closed again, the staff-sergeant was in the room alone with Kent. In one of his big hands he clutched a box of cigars, and in the other he held a bunch of vividly red fire-flowers.

"Father Layonne shoved these into my hands as I was coming up," he explained, dropping them on the table. "And I—well—I'm breaking regulations to come up an' tell you something, Jimmy. I never called you a liar in my life, but I'm calling you one now!"

He was gripping Kent's hands in the fierce clasp of a friendship that nothing could kill. Kent winced, but the pain of it was joy. He had feared that O'Connor, like Kedsty, must of necessity turn against him. Then he noticed something unusual in O'Connor's face and eyes. The staff-sergeant was not easily excited, yet he was visibly disturbed now.

"I don't know what the others saw, when you were making that confession, Kent. Mebby my eyesight was better because I spent a year and a half with you on the trail. You were lying. What's your game, old man?"

Kent groaned. "Have I got to go all over it again?" he appealed.

O'Connor began thumping back and forth over the floor. Kent had seen him that way sometimes in camp when there were perplexing problems ahead of them.

"You didn't kill John Barkley," he insisted. "I don't believe you did, and Inspector Kedsty doesn't believe it—yet the mighty queer part of it is—"

"What?"

"That Kedsty is acting on your confession in a big hurry. I don't believe it's according to Hoyle, as the regulations are written. But he's doing it. And I want to know—it's the biggest thing I EVER wanted to know—did you kill Barkley?"

"O'Connor, if you don't believe a dying man's word—you haven't much respect for death, have you?"

"That's the theory on which the law works, but sometimes it ain't human. Confound it, man, *did you?*"

"Yes."

O'Connor sat down and with his finger-nails pried open the box of cigars. "Mind if I smoke with you?" he asked. "I need it. I'm shot up with unexpected things this morning. Do you care if I ask you about the girl?"

"The girl!" exclaimed Kent. He sat up straighter, staring at O'Connor.

The staff-sergeant's eyes were on him with questioning steadiness. "I see— you don't know her," he said, lighting his cigar. "Neither do I. Never saw her before. That's why I am wondering about Inspector Kedsty. I tell you, it's queer. He didn't believe you this morning, yet he was all shot up. He wanted me to go with him to his house. The cords stood out on his neck like that— like my little finger.

"Then suddenly he changed his mind and said we'd go to the office. That took us along the road that runs through the poplar grove. It happened there. I'm not much of a girl's man, Kent, and I'd be a fool to try to tell you what she looked like. But there she was, standing in the path not ten feet ahead of us, and she stopped me in my tracks as quick as though she'd sent a shot into me. And she stopped Kedsty, too. I heard him give a sort of grunt—a funny sound, as though some one had hit him. I don't believe I could tell whether she had a dress on or not, for I never saw anything like her face, and her eyes, and her hair, and I stared at them like a thunder-struck fool. She didn't seem to notice me any more than if I'd been thin air, a ghost she couldn't see.

"She looked straight at Kedsty, and she kept looking at him—and then she passed us. Never said a word, mind you. She came so near I could have touched her with my hand, and not until she was that close did she take her eyes from Kedsty and look at me. And when she'd passed I thought what a couple of cursed idiots we were, standing there paralyzed, as if we'd never seen a beautiful girl before in our lives. I went to remark that much to the Old Man when—"

O'Connor bit his cigar half in two as he leaned nearer to the cot.

"Kent, I swear that Kedsty was as white as chalk when I looked at him! There wasn't a drop of blood left in his face, and he was staring straight ahead, as though the girl still stood there, and he gave another of those grunts—it wasn't a laugh—as if something was choking him. And then he said:

"'Sergeant, I've forgotten something important. I must go back to see Dr. Cardigan. You have my authority to give McTrigger his liberty at once!'"

O'Connor paused, as if expecting some expression of disbelief from Kent. When none came, he demanded,

"Was that according to the Criminal Code? Was it, Kent?"

"Not exactly. But, coming from the S.O.D., it was law."

"And I obeyed it," grunted the staff-sergeant. "And if you could have seen McTrigger! When I told him he was free, and unlocked his cell, he came out of it gropingly, like a blind man. And he would go no farther than the Inspector's office. He said he would wait there for him."

"And Kedsty?"

O'Connor jumped from his chair and began thumping back and forth across the room again. "Followed the girl," he exploded. "He couldn't have done anything else. He lied to me about Cardigan. There wouldn't be anything mysterious about it if he wasn't sixty and she less than twenty. She was pretty enough! But it wasn't her beauty that made him turn white there in the path. Not on your life it wasn't! I tell you he aged ten years in as many seconds. There was something in that girl's eyes more terrifying to him than a leveled gun, and after he'd looked into them, his first thought was of McTrigger, the man you're saving from the hangman. It's queer, Kent. The whole business is queer. And the queerest of it all is your confession."

"Yes, it's all very funny," agreed Kent. "That's what I've been telling myself right along, old man. You see, a little thing like a bullet changed it all. For if the bullet hadn't got me, I assure you I wouldn't have given Kedsty that confession, and an innocent man would have been hanged. As it is, Kedsty is shocked, demoralized. I'm the first man to soil the honor of the finest Service on the face of the earth, and I'm in Kedsty's division. Quite natural that he should be upset. And as for the girl—"

He shrugged his shoulders and tried to laugh. "Perhaps she came in this morning with one of the up-river scows and was merely taking a little constitutional," he suggested. "Didn't you ever notice, O'Connor, that in a certain light under poplar trees one's face is sometimes ghastly?"

"Yes, I've noticed it, when the trees are in full leaf, but not when they're just opening, Jimmy. It was the girl. Her eyes shattered every nerve in him. And his first words were an order for me to free McTrigger, coupled with the lie that he was coming back to see Cardigan. And if you could have seen her eyes when she turned them on me! They were blue—blue as violets—but shooting fire. I could imagine black eyes like that, but not blue ones. Kedsty simply wilted in their blaze. And there was a reason—I know it—a reason that sent his mind like lightning to the man in the cell!"

"Now, that you leave me out of it, the thing begins to get interesting," said Kent. "It's a matter of the relationship of this blonde girl and—"

"She isn't blonde—and I'm not leaving you out of it," interrupted O'Connor. "I never saw anything so black in my life as her hair. It was magnificent. If you saw that girl once, you would never forget her again as long as you lived. She has never been in Athabasca Landing before, or anywhere near here. If she had, we surely would have heard about her. She came for a purpose, and I believe that purpose was accomplished when Kedsty gave me the order to free McTrigger."

"That's possible, and probable," agreed Kent. "I always said you were the best clue-analyst in the force, Bucky. But I don't see where I come in."

O'Connor smiled grimly. "You don't? Well, I may be both blind and a fool, and perhaps a little excited. But it seemed to me that from the moment Inspector Kedsty laid his eyes on that girl he was a little too anxious to let McTrigger go and hang you in his place. A little too anxious, Kent."

The irony of the thing brought a hard smile to Kent's lips as he nodded for the cigars. "I'll try one of these on top of the pipe," he said, nipping off the end of the cigar with his teeth. "And you forget that I'm not going to hang, Bucky. Cardigan has given me until tomorrow night. Perhaps until the next day. Did you see Rossand's fleet leaving for up north? It made me think of three years ago!"

O'Connor was gripping his hand again. The coldness of it sent a chill into the staff-sergeant's heart. He rose and looked through the upper part of the window, so that the twitching in his throat was hidden from Kent. Then he went to the door.

"I'll see you again tomorrow," he said. "And if I find out anything more about the girl, I'll report."

He tried to laugh, but there was a tremble in his voice, a break in the humor he attempted to force.

Kent listened to the tramp of his heavy feet as they went down the hall.

CHAPTER III

Again the world came back to Kent, the world that lay just beyond his open window. But scarcely had O'Connor gone when it began to change, and in spite of his determination to keep hold of his nerve Kent felt creeping up with that change a thing that was oppressive and smothering. Swiftly the distant billowings of the forests were changing their tones and colors under the darkening approach of storm. The laughter of the hills and ridges went out. The shimmer of spruce and cedar and balsam turned to a somber black. The flashing gold and silver of birch and poplar dissolved into a ghostly and unanimated gray that was almost invisible. A deepening and somber gloom spread itself like a veil over the river that only a short time before had reflected the glory of the sun in the faces of dark-visaged men of the Company brigade. And with the gloom came steadily nearer a low rumbling of thunder.

For the first time since the mental excitement of his confession Kent felt upon him an appalling loneliness. He still was not afraid of death, but a part of his philosophy was gone. It was, after all, a difficult thing to die alone. He felt that the pressure in his chest was perceptible greater than it had been an hour or two before, and the thought grew upon him that it would be a terrible thing for the "explosion" to come when the sun was not shining. He wanted O'Connor back again. He had the desire to call out for Cardigan. He would have welcomed Father Layonne with a glad cry. Yet more than all else would he have had at his side in these moments of distress a woman. For the storm, as it massed heavier and nearer, filling the earth with its desolation, bridged vast spaces for him, and he found himself suddenly face to face with the might-have-beens of yesterday.

He saw, as he had never guessed before, the immeasurable gulf between helplessness and the wild, brute freedom of man, and his soul cried out—not for adventure, not for the savage strength of life—but for the presence of a creature frailer than himself, yet in the gentle touch of whose hand lay the might of all humanity.

He struggled with himself. He remembered that Dr. Cardigan had told him there would be moments of deep depression, and he tried to fight himself out of the grip of this that was on him. There was a bell at hand, but he refused to use it, for he sensed his own cowardice. His cigar had gone out, and he relighted it. He made an effort to bring his mind back to O'Connor, and the mystery girl, and Kedsty. He tried to visualize McTrigger, the man he had saved from the hangman, waiting for Kedsty in the office at barracks. He pictured the girl, as O'Connor had described her, with her black hair and blue eyes—and then the storm broke.

The rain came down in a deluge, and scarcely had it struck when the door opened and Cardigan hurried in to close the window. He remained for half an hour, and after that young Mercer, one of his two assistants, came in at intervals. Late in the afternoon it began to clear up, and Father Layonne returned with papers properly made out for Kent's signature. He was with Kent until sundown, when Mercer came in with supper.

Between that hour and ten o'clock Kent observed a vigilance on the part of Dr. Cardigan which struck him as being unusual. Four times he listened with the stethoscope at his chest, but when Kent asked the question which was in his mind, Cardigan shook his head.

"It's no worse, Kent. I don't think it will happen tonight."

In spite of this assurance Kent was positive there was in Cardigan's manner an anxiety of a different quality than he had perceived earlier in the day. The thought was a definite and convincing one. He believed that Cardigan was smoothing the way with a professional lie.

He had no desire to sleep. His light was turned low, and his window was open again, for the night had cleared. Never had air tasted sweeter to him than that which came in through his window. The little bell in his watch tinkled the hour of eleven, when he heard Cardigan's door close for a last time across the hall. After that everything was quiet. He drew himself nearer to the window, so that by leaning forward he could rest himself partly on the sill. He loved the night. The mystery and lure of those still hours of darkness when the world slept had never ceased to hold their fascination for him. Night and he were friends. He had discovered many of its secrets. A thousand times he had walked hand in hand with the spirit of it, approaching each time a little nearer to the heart of it, mastering its life, its sound, the whispering languages of that "other side of life" which rises quietly and as if in fear to live and breathe long after the sun has gone out. To him it was more wonderful than day.

And this night that lay outside his window now was magnificent. Storm had washed the atmosphere between earth and sky, and it seemed as though the stars had descended nearer to his forests, shining in golden constellations. The moon was coming up late, and he watched the ruddy glow of it as it rode up over the wilderness, a splendid queen entering upon a stage already prepared by the lesser satellites for her coming. No longer was Kent oppressed or afraid. In still deeper inhalations he drank the night air into his lungs, and in him there seemed to grow slowly a new strength. His eyes and ears were wide open and attentive. The town was asleep, but a few lights burned dimly here and there along the river's edge, and occasionally a lazy sound came up to him—the clink of a scow chain, the bark of a dog, the rooster crowing. In spite of himself he smiled at that. Old Duperow's rooster was a foolish bird and always crowed himself hoarse when the moon was bright. And in front of him, not far away, were two white, lightning-shriven spruce stubs standing like ghosts in the night. In one of these a pair of owls had nested, and Kent listened to the queer, chuckling notes of their honeymooning and the flutter of their wings as they darted out now and then in play close to his window. And then suddenly he heard the sharp snap of their beaks. An enemy was prowling near, and the owls were giving warning. He thought he heard a step. In another moment or two the step was unmistakable. Some one was approaching his window from the end of the building. He leaned over the sill and found himself staring into O'Connor's face.

"These confounded feet of mine!" grunted the staff-sergeant. "Were you asleep, Kent?"

"Wide-awake as those owls," assured Kent.

O'Connor drew up to the window. "I saw your light and thought you were awake," he said. "I wanted to make sure Cardigan wasn't with you. I don't want him to know I am here. And—if you don't mind—will you turn off the light? Kedsty is awake, too—as wide-awake as the owls."

Kent reached out a hand, and his room was in darkness except for the glow of moon and stars. O'Connor's bulk at the window shut out a part of this. His face was half in gloom.

"It's a crime to come to you like this, Kent," he said, keeping his big voice down to a whisper. "But I had to. It's my last chance. And I know there's something wrong. Kedsty is getting me out of the way—because I was with him when he met the girl over in the poplar bush. I'm detailed on special duty up at Fort Simpson, two thousand miles by water if it's a foot! It means six months or a year. We leave in the motor boat at dawn to overtake Rossand and his outfit, so I had to take this chance of seeing you. I hesitated until I knew that some one was awake in your room."

"I'm glad you came," said Kent warmly. "And—good God, how I would like to go with you, Bucky! If it wasn't for this thing in my chest, ballooning up for an explosion—"

"I wouldn't be going," interrupted O'Connor in a low voice. "If you were on your feet, Kent, there are a number of things that wouldn't be happening. Something mighty queer has come over Kedsty since this morning. He isn't the Kedsty you knew yesterday or for the last ten years. He's nervous, and I miss my guess if he isn't constantly on the watch for some one. And he's afraid of me. I know it. He's afraid of me because I saw him go to pieces when he met that girl. Fort Simpson is simply a frame-up to get me away for a time. He tried to smooth the edge off the thing by promising me an inspectorship within the year. That was this afternoon, just before the storm. Since then—"

O'Connor turned and faced the moonlight for a moment.

"Since then I've been on a still-hunt for the girl and Sandy McTrigger," he added. "And they've disappeared, Kent. I guess McTrigger just melted away into the woods. But it's the girl that puzzles me. I've questioned every scow *cheman* at the Landing. I've investigated every place where she might have got food or lodging, and I bribed Mooie, the old trailer, to search the near-by timber. The unbelievable part of it isn't her disappearance. It's the fact that not a soul in Athabasca Landing has seen her! Sounds incredible, doesn't it? And then, Kent, the big hunch came to me. Remember how we've always played up to the big hunch? And this one struck me strong. I think I know where the girl is."

Kent, forgetful of his own impending doom, was deeply interested in the thrill of O'Connor's mystery. He had begun to visualize the situation. More than once they had worked out enigmas of this kind together, and the staff-sergeant saw the old, eager glow in his eyes. And Kent chuckled joyously in that thrill of the game of man-hunting, and said:

"Kedsty is a bachelor and doesn't even so much as look at a woman. But he likes home life—"

"And has built himself a log bungalow somewhat removed from the town," added O'Connor.

"And his Chinaman cook and housekeeper is away."

"And the bungalow is closed, or supposed to be."

"Except at night, when Kedsty goes there to sleep."

O'Connor's hand gripped Kent's. "Jimmy, there never was a team in N Division that could beat us, The girl is hiding at Kedsty's place!"

"But why *hiding*?" insisted Kent. "She hasn't committed a crime."

O'Connor sat silent for a moment. Kent could hear him stuffing the bowl of his pipe.

"It's simply the big hunch," he grunted. "It's got hold of me, Kent, and I can't throw it off. Why, man—"

He lighted a match in the cup of his hands, and Kent saw his face. There was more than uncertainty in the hard, set lines of it.

"You see, I went back to the poplars again after I left you today," O'Connor went on. "I found her footprints. She had turned off the trail, and in places they were very clear.

"She had on high-heeled shoes, Kent—those Frenchy things—and I swear her feet can't be much bigger than a baby's! I found where Kedsty caught up with her, and the moss was pretty well beaten down. He returned through the poplars, but the girl went on and into the edge of the spruce. I lost her trail there. By traveling in that timber it was possible for her to reach Kedsty's bungalow without being seen. It must have been difficult going, with shoes half as big as my hand and heels two inches high! And I've been wondering, why didn't she wear bush-country shoes or moccasins?"

"Because she came from the South and not the North," suggested Kent. "Probably up from Edmonton."

"Exactly. And Kedsty wasn't expecting her, was he? If he had been, that first sight of her wouldn't have shattered every nerve in his body. That's why the big hunch won't let loose of me, Kent. From the moment he saw her, he was a different man. His attitude toward you changed instantly. If he could save you now by raising his little finger, he wouldn't do it, simply because it's absolutely necessary for him to have an excuse for freeing McTrigger. Your confession came at just the psychological moment. The girl's unspoken demand there in the poplars was that he free McTrigger, and it was backed up by a threat which Kedsty understood and which terrified him to his marrow. McTrigger must have seen him afterward, for he waited at the office until Kedsty came. I don't know what passed between them. Constable Doyle says they were together for half an hour. Then McTrigger walked out of barracks, and no one has seen him since. It's mighty queer. The whole thing is queer. And the queerest part of the whole business is this sudden commission of mine at Fort Simpson."

Kent leaned back against his pillows. His breath came in a series of short, hacking coughs. In the star glow O'Connor saw his face grow suddenly haggard and tired-looking, and he leaned far in so that in both his own hands he held one of Kent's.

"I'm tiring you, Jimmy," he said huskily. "Good-by, old pal! I—I—" He hesitated and then lied steadily. "I'm going up to take a look around Kedsty's place. I won't be gone more than half an hour and will stop on my way back. If you're asleep—"

"I won't be asleep," said Kent.

O'Connor's hands gripped closer. "Good-by, Jimmy."

"Good-by." And then, as O'Connor stepped back into the night, Kent's voice called after him softly: "I'll be with you on the long trip, Bucky. Take care of yourself—always."

O'Connor's answer was a sob, a sob that rose in his throat like a great fist, and choked him, and filled his eyes with scalding tears that shut out the glow of moon and stars. And he did not go toward Kedsty's, but trudged heavily in the direction of the river, for he knew that Kent had called his lie, and that they had said their last farewell.

CHAPTER IV

It was a long time after O'Connor had gone before Kent at last fell asleep. It was a slumber weighted with the restlessness of a brain fighting to the last against exhaustion and the inevitable end. A strange spirit seemed whirling Kent back through the years he had lived, even to the days of his boyhood, leaping from crest to crest, giving to him swift and passing visions of valleys almost forgotten, of happenings and things long ago faded and indistinct in his memory. Vividly his dreams were filled with ghosts—ghosts that were transformed, as his spirit went back to them, until they were riotous with life and pulsating with the red blood of reality. He was a boy again, playing three-old-cat in front of the little old red brick schoolhouse half a mile from the farm where he was born, and where his mother had died.

And Skinny Hill, dead many years ago, was his partner at the bat—lovable Skinny, with his smirking grin and his breath that always smelled of the most delicious onions ever raised in Ohio. And then, at dinner hour, he was trading some of his mother's cucumber pickles for some of Skinny's onions—two onions for a pickle, and never a change in the price. And he played old-fashioned casino with his mother, and they were picking blackberries together in the woods, and he killed over again a snake that he had clubbed to death more than twenty years ago, while his mother ran away and screamed and then sat down and cried.

He had worshiped that mother, and the spirit of his dreams did not let him look down into the valley where she lay dead, under a little white stone in the country cemetery a thousand miles away, with his father close beside her. But it gave him a passing thrill of the days in which he had fought his way through college—and then it brought him into the North, his beloved North.

For hours the wilderness was heavy about Kent. He moved restlessly, at times he seemed about to awaken, but always he slipped back into the slumberous arms of his forests. He was on the trail in the cold, gray beginning of Winter, and the glow of his campfire made a radiant patch of red glory in the heart of the night, and close to him in that glow sat O'Connor. He was behind dogs and sledge, fighting storm; dark and mysterious streams rippled under his canoe; he was on the Big River, O'Connor with him again—and then, suddenly, he was holding a blazing gun in his hand, and he and O'Connor stood with their backs to a rack, facing the bloodthirsty rage of McCaw and his free-traders. The roar of the guns half roused him, and after that came pleasanter things—the droning of wind in the spruce tops, the singing of swollen streams in Springtime, the songs of birds, the sweet smells of life, the glory of life as he had lived it, he and O'Connor. In the end, half between sleep and wakefulness, he was fighting a smothering pressure on his chest. It was an oppressive and torturing thing, like the tree that had fallen on him over in the Jackfish country, and he felt himself slipping off into darkness. Suddenly there was a gleam of light. He opened his eyes. The sun was flooding in at his window, and the weight on his chest was the gentle pressure of Cardigan's stethoscope.

In spite of the physical stress of the phantoms which his mind has conceived, Kent awakened so quietly that Cardigan was not conscious of the fact until he raised his head. There was something in his face which he tried to conceal, but Kent caught it before it was gone. There were dark hollows under his eyes. He was a bit haggard, as though he had spent a sleepless night. Kent pulled himself up, squinting at the sun and grinning apologetically. He had slept well along into the day, and—

He caught himself with a sudden grimace of pain. A flash of something hot and burning swept through his chest. It was like a knife. He opened his mouth to breathe in the air. The pressure inside him was no longer the pressure of a stethoscope. It was real.

Cardigan, standing over him, was trying to look cheerful. "Too much of the night air, Kent," he explained. "That will pass away—soon."

It seemed to Kent that Cardigan gave an almost imperceptible emphasis to the word "soon," but he asked no question. He was quite sure that he understood, and he knew how unpleasant for Cardigan the answer to it would be. He fumbled under his pillow for his watch. It was nine o'clock. Cardigan was moving about uneasily, arranging the things on the table and adjusting the shade at the window. For a few moments, with his back to Kent, he stood without moving. Then he turned, and said:

"Which will you have, Kent—a wash-up and breakfast, or a visitor?"

"I am not hungry, and I don't feel like soap and water just now. Who's the visitor? Father Layonne or—Kedsty?"

"Neither. It's a lady."

"Then I'd better have the soap and water! Do you mind telling me who it is?"

Cardigan shook his head. "I don't know. I've never seen her before. She came this morning while I was still in pajamas, and has been waiting ever since. I told her to come back again, but she insisted that she would remain until you were awake. She has been very patient for two hours."

A thrill which he made no effort to conceal leaped through Kent. "Is she a young woman?" he demanded eagerly. "Wonderful black hair, blue eyes, wears high-heeled shoes just about half as big as your hand—and very beautiful?"

"All of that," nodded Cardigan. "I even noticed the shoes, Jimmy. A very beautiful young woman!"

"Please let her come in," said Kent. "Mercer scrubbed me last night, and I feel fairly fit. She'll forgive this beard, and I'll apologize for your sake. What is her name?"

"I asked her, and she didn't seem to hear. A little later Mercer asked her, and he said she just looked at him for a moment and he froze. She is reading a volume of my Plutarch's 'Lives'—actually reading it. I know it by the way she turns the pages!"

Kent drew himself up higher against his pillows and faced the door when Cardigan went out. In a flash all that O'Connor had said swept back upon him—this girl, Kedsty, the mystery of it all. Why had she come to see him? What could be the motive of her visit—unless it was to thank him for the confession that had given Sandy McTrigger his freedom? O'Connor was right. She was deeply concerned in McTrigger and had come to express her gratitude. He listened. Distant footsteps sounded in the hall. They approached quickly and paused outside his door. A hand moved the latch, but for a moment the door did not open. He heard Cardigan's voice, then Cardigan's footsteps retreating down the hall. His heart thumped. He could not remember when he had been so upset over an unimportant thing.

CHAPTER V

The latch moved slowly, and with its movement came a gentle tap on the panel.

"Come in," he said.

The next instant he was staring. The girl had entered and closed the door behind her. O'Connor's picture stood in flesh and blood before him. The girl's eyes met his own. They were like glorious violets, as O'Connor had said, but they were not the eyes he had expected to see. They were the wide-open, curious eyes of a child. He had visualized them as pools of slumbering flame—the idea O'Connor had given him—and they were the opposite of that. Their one emotion seemed to be the emotion roused by an overwhelming, questioning curiosity. They were apparently not regarding him as a dying human being, but as a creature immensely interesting to look upon. In place of the gratitude he had anticipated, they were filled with a great, wondering interrogation, and there was not the slightest hint of embarrassment in their gaze. For a space it seemed to Kent that he saw nothing but those wonderful, dispassionate eyes looking at him. Then he saw the rest of her—her amazing hair, her pale, exquisite face, the slimness and beauty of her as she stood with her back to the door, one hand still resting on the latch. He had never seen anything quite like her. He might have guessed that she was eighteen, or twenty, or twenty-two. Her hair, wreathed in shimmering, velvety coils from the back to the crown of her head, struck him as it had struck O'Connor, as unbelievable. The glory of it gave to her an appearance of height which she did not possess, for she was not tall, and her slimness added to the illusion.

And then, greatly to his embarrassment in the next instant, his eyes went to her feet. Again O'Connor was right—tiny feet, high-heeled pumps, ravishingly turned ankles showing under a skirt of some fluffy brown stuff or other—

Correcting himself, his face flushed red. The faintest tremble of a smile was on the girl's lips. She looked down, and for the first time he saw what O'Connor had seen, the sunlight kindling slumberous fires in her hair.

Kent tried to say something, but before he succeeded she had taken possession of the chair near his bedside.

"I have been waiting a long time to see you," she said. "You are James Kent, aren't you?"

"Yes, I'm Jim Kent. I'm sorry Dr. Cardigan kept you waiting. If I had known—"

He was getting a grip on himself again, and smiled at her. He noticed the amazing length of her dark lashes, but the violet eyes behind them did not smile back at him. The tranquillity of their gaze was disconcerting. It was as if she had not quite made up her mind about him yet and was still trying to classify him in the museum of things she had known.

"He should have awakened me," Kent went on, trying to keep himself from slipping once more. "It isn't polite to keep a young lady waiting two hours!"

This time the blue eyes made him feel that his smile was a maudlin grin.

"Yes—you are different." She spoke softly, as if expressing the thought to herself. "That is what I came to find out, if you were different. You are dying?"

"My God—yes—I'm dying!" gasped Kent. "According to Dr. Cardigan I'm due to pop off this minute. Aren't you a little nervous, sitting so near to a man who's ready to explode while you're looking at him?"

For the first time the eyes changed. She was not facing the window, yet a glow like the glow of sunlight flashed into them, soft, luminous, almost laughing.

"No, it doesn't frighten me," she assured him. "I have always thought I should like to see a man die—not quickly, like drowning or being shot, but slowly, an inch at a time. But I shouldn't like to see YOU die."

"I'm glad," breathed Kent. "It's a great satisfaction to me."

"Yet I shouldn't be frightened if you did."

"Oh!"

Kent drew himself up straighter against his pillows. He had been a man of many adventures. He had faced almost every conceivable kind of shock. But this was a new one. He stared into the blue eyes, tongueless and mentally dazed. They were cool and sweet and not at all excited. And he knew that she spoke the truth. Not by a quiver of those lovely lashes would she betray either fear or horror if he popped off right there. It was astonishing.

Something like resentment shot for an instant into his bewildered brain. Then it was gone, and in a flash it came upon him that she was but uttering his own philosophy of life, showing him life's cheapness, life's littleness, the absurdity of being distressed by looking upon the light as it flickered out. And she was doing it, not as a philosopher, but with the beautiful unconcern of a child.

Suddenly, as if impelled by an emotion in direct contradiction to her apparent lack of sympathy, she reached out a hand and placed it on Kent's forehead.

It was another shock. It was not a professional touch, but a soft, cool little pressure that sent a comforting thrill through him. The hand was there for only a moment, and she withdrew it to entwine the slim fingers with those of the others in her lap.

"You have no fever," she said. "What makes you think you are dying?"

Kent explained what was happening inside him. He was completely shunted off his original track of thought and anticipation. He had expected to ask for at least a mutual introduction when his visitor came into his room, and had anticipated taking upon himself the position of a polite inquisitor. In spite of O'Connor, he had not thought she would be quite so pretty. He had not believed her eyes would be so beautiful, or their lashes so long, or the touch of her hand so pleasantly unnerving. And now, in place of asking for her name and the reason for her visit, he became an irrational idiot, explaining to her certain matters of physiology that had to do with aortas and aneurismal sacs. He had finished before the absurdity of the situation dawned upon him, and with absurdity came the humor of it. Even dying, Kent could not fail to see the funny side of a thing It struck him as suddenly as had the girl's beauty and her bewildering and unaffected ingenuousness.

Looking at him, that same glow of mysterious questioning in her eyes, the girl found him suddenly laughing straight into her face.

"This is funny. It's very funny, Miss—Miss—"

"Marette," she supplied, answering his hesitation.

"It's funny, Miss Marette."

"Not Miss Marette. Just Marette," she corrected.

"I say, it's funny," he tried again. "You see, it's not so terribly pleasant as you might think to—er—be here, where I am, dying. And last night I thought about the finest thing in the world would be to have a woman beside me, a woman who'd be sort of sympathetic, you know, ease the thing off a little, maybe say she was sorry. And then the Lord answers my prayer, and *you* come—and you sort of give me the impression that you made the appointment with yourself to see how a fellow looks when he pops off."

The shimmer of light came into the blue eyes again. She seemed to have done with her mental analysis of him, and he saw that a bit of color was creeping into her cheeks, pale when she had entered the room.

"You wouldn't be the first I've seen pop off," she assured him. "There have been a number, and I've never cried very much. I'd rather see a man die than some animals. But I shouldn't like to see YOU do it. Does that comfort you—like the woman you prayed the Lord for?"

"It does," gasped Kent. "But why the devil, Miss Marette—"

"Marette," she corrected again.

"Yes, Marette—why the devil have you come to see me at just the moment I'm due to explode? And what's your other name, and how old are you, and what do you want of me?"

"I haven't any other name, I'm twenty, and I came to get acquainted with you and see what you are like."

"Bully!" exclaimed Kent. "We're getting there fast! And now, why?"

The girl drew her chair a few inches nearer, and for a moment Kent thought that her lovely mouth was trembling on the edge of a smile.

"Because you have lied so splendidly to save another man who was about to die."

"*Et tu, Brute!*" sighed Kent, leaning back against his pillows. "Isn't it possible for a decent man to kill another man and not be called a liar when he tells about it? Why do so many believe that I lie?"

"They don't," said the girl. "They believe you—now. You have gone so completely into the details of the murder in your confession that they are quite convinced. It would be too bad if you lived, for you surely would be hanged. Your lie sounds and reads like the truth. But I know it is a lie. You did not kill John Barkley."

"And the reason for your suspicion?"

For fully half a minute the girl's eyes rested on, his own. Again they seemed to be looking through him and into him. "Because I know the man who DID kill him," she said quietly, "and it was not you."

Kent made a mighty effort to appear calm. He reached for a cigar from the box that Cardigan had placed on his bed, and nibbled the end of it. "Has some one else been confessing?" he asked.

She shook her head the slightest bit.

"Did you—er—see this other gentleman kill John Barkley?" he insisted.

"No."

"Then I must answer you as I have answered at least one other. I killed John Barkley. If you suspect some other person, your suspicion is wrong."

"What a splendid liar!" she breathed softly. "Don't you believe in God?"

Kent winced. "In a large, embracing sense, yes," he said. "I believe in Him, for instance, as revealed to our senses in all that living, growing glory you see out there through the window Nature and I have become pretty good pals, and you see I've sort of built up a mother goddess to worship instead of a he-god. Sacrilege, maybe, but it's a great comfort at times. But you didn't come to talk religion?"

The lovely head bent still nearer him. He felt an impelling desire to put up his hand and touch her shining hair, as she laid her hand on his forehead.

"I know who killed John Barkley," she insisted. "I know how and when and why he was killed. Please tell me the truth. I want to know. Why did you confess to a crime which you did not commit?"

Kent took time to light his cigar. The girl watched him closely, almost eagerly.

"I may be mad," he said. "It is possible for any human being to be mad and not know it. That's the funny part about insanity. But if I'm not insane, I killed Barkley; if I didn't kill him, I must be insane, for I'm very well convinced that I did. Either that, or you are insane. I have my suspicions that you are. Would a sane person wear pumps with heels like those up here?" He pointed accusingly to the floor.

For the first time the girl smiled, openly, frankly, gloriously. It was as if her heart had leaped forth for an instant and had greeted him. And then, like sunlight shadowed by cloud, the smile was gone. "You are a brave man," she said. "You are splendid. I hate men. But I think if you lived very long, I should love you. I will believe that you killed Barkley. You compel me to believe it. You confessed, when you found you were going to die, that an innocent man might be saved. Wasn't that it?"

Kent nodded weakly. "That's it. I hate to think of it that way, but I guess it's true. I confessed because I knew I was going to die. Otherwise I am quite sure that I should have let the other fellow take my medicine for me. You must think I am a beast."

"All men are beasts," she agreed quickly. "But you are—a different kind of beast. I like you. If there were a chance, I might fight for you. I can fight." She held up her two small hands, half smiling at him again.

"But not with those," he exclaimed. "I think you would fight with your eyes. O'Connor told me they half killed Kedsty when you met them in the poplar grove yesterday."

He had expected that the mention of Inspector Kedsty's name would disturb her. It had no effect that he could perceive.

"O'Connor was the big, red-faced man with Mr. Kedsty?"

"Yes, my trail partner. He came to me yesterday and raved about your eyes. They ARE beautiful; I've never seen eyes half so lovely. But that wasn't what struck Bucky so hard. It was the effect they had on Kedsty. He said they shattered every nerve in Kedsty's body, and Kedsty isn't the sort to get easily frightened. And the queer part of it was that the instant you had gone, he gave O'Connor an order to free McTrigger—and then turned and followed you. All the rest of that day O'Connor tried to discover something about you at the Landing. He couldn't find hide nor hair—I beg pardon!—I mean he couldn't find out anything about you at all. We made up our minds that for some reason or other you were hiding up at Kedsty's bungalow. You don't mind a fellow saying all this—when he is going to pop off soon—do you?"

He was half frightened at the directness with which he had expressed the thing. He would gladly have buried his own curiosity and all of O'Connor's suspicions for another moment of her hand on his forehead. But it was out, and he waited.

She was looking down, her fingers twisting some sort of tasseled dress ornament in her lap, and Kent mentally measured the length of her lashes with a foot rule in mind. They were superb, and in the thrill of his admiration he would have sworn they were an inch long. She looked up suddenly and caught the glow in his eyes and the flush that lay under the tan of his cheeks. Her own color had deepened a little.

"What if you shouldn't die?" she asked him bluntly, as if she had not heard a word of all he had said about Kedsty. "What would you do?"

"I'm going to."

"But if you shouldn't?"

Kent shrugged his shoulders. "I suppose I'd have to take my medicine. You're not going?"

She had straightened up and was sitting on the edge of her chair. "Yes, I'm going. I'm afraid of my eyes. I may look at you as I looked at Mr. Kedsty, and then—pop you'd go, quick! And I don't want to be here when you die!"

He heard a soft little note of laughter in her throat. It sent a chill through him. What an adorable, blood-thirsty little wretch she was! He stared at her bent head, at the shining coils of her wonderful hair. Undone, he could see it completely hiding her. And it was so soft and warm that again he was tempted to reach out and touch it. She was wonderful, and yet it was not possible that she had a heart. Her apparent disregard of the fact that he was a dying man was almost diabolic. There was no sympathy in the expression of her violet eyes as she looked at him. She was even making fun of the fact that he was about to die!

She stood up, surveying for the first time the room in which she had been sitting. Then she turned to the window and looked out. She reminded Kent of a beautiful young willow that had grown at the edge of a stream, exquisite, slender, strong. He could have picked her up in his arms as easily as a child, yet he sensed in the lithe beauty of her body forces that could endure magnificently. The careless poise of her head fascinated him. For that head and the hair that crowned it he knew that half the women of the earth would have traded precious years of their lives.

And then, without turning toward him, she said, "Some day, when I die, I wish I might have as pleasant a room as this."

"I hope you never die," he replied devoutly.

She came back and stood for a moment beside him.

"I have had a very pleasant time," she said, as though he had given her a special sort of entertainment. "It's too bad you are going to die. I'm sure we should have been good friends. Aren't you?"

"Yes, very sure. If you had only arrived sooner—"

"And I shall always think of you as a different kind of man-beast," she interrupted him. "It is really true that I shouldn't like to see you die. I want to get away before it happens. Would you care to have me kiss you?"

For an instant Kent felt that his aorta was about to give away. "I—I would," he gasped huskily.

"Then—close your eyes, please."

He obeyed. She bent over him. He felt the soft touch of her hands and caught for an instant the perfume of her face and hair, and then the thrill of her lips pressed warm and soft upon his.

She was not flushed or embarrassed when he looked at her again. It was as if she had kissed a baby and was wondering at its red face. "I've only kissed three men before you," she avowed. "It is strange. I never thought I should do it again. And now, good-by!" She moved quickly to the door.

"Wait," he cried plaintively. "Please wait. I want to know your name. It is Marette—"

"Radisson," she finished for him. "Marette Radisson, and I come from away off there, from a place we call the Valley of Silent Men." She was pointing into the north.

"The North!" he exclaimed.

"Yes, it is far north. Very far."

Her hand was on the latch. The door opened slowly.

"Wait," he pleaded again. "You must not go."

"Yes, I must go. I have remained too long. I am sorry I kissed you. I shouldn't have done that. But I had to because you are such a splendid liar!"

The door opened quickly and closed behind her. He heard her steps almost running down the hall, where not long ago he had listened to the last of O'Connor's.

And then there was silence, and in that silence he heard her words again, drumming like little hammers in his head, *Because you are such a splendid liar!*"

CHAPTER VI

James Kent, among his other qualities good and bad, possessed a merciless opinion of his own shortcomings, but never, in that opinion, had he fallen so low as in the interval which immediately followed the closing of his door behind the mysterious girl who had told him that her name was Marette Radisson. No sooner was she gone than the overwhelming superiority of her childlike cleverness smote him until, ashamed of himself, he burned red in his aloneness.

He, Sergeant Kent, the coolest man on the force next to Inspector Kedsty, the most dreaded of catechists when questioning criminals, the man who had won the reputation of facing quietly and with deadly sureness the most menacing of dangers, had been beaten—horribly beaten—by a girl! And yet, in defeat, an irrepressible and at times distorted sense of humor made him give credit to the victor. The shame of the thing was his acknowledgment that a bit of feminine beauty had done the trick. He had made fun of O'Connor when the big staff-sergeant had described the effect of the girl's eyes on Inspector Kedsty. And, now, if O'Connor could know of what had happened here—

And then, like a rubber ball, that saving sense of humor bounced up out of the mess, and Kent found himself chuckling as his face grew cooler. His visitor had come, and she had gone, and he knew no more about her than when she had entered his room, except that her very pretty name was Marette Radisson. He was just beginning to think of the questions he had wanted to ask, a dozen, half a hundred of them—more definitely who she was; how and why she had come to Athabasca Landing; her interest in Sandy McTrigger; the mysterious relationship that must surely exist between her and Inspector Kedsty; and, chiefly, her real motive in coming to him when she knew that he was dying. He comforted himself by the assurance that he would have learned these things had she not left him so suddenly. He had not expected that.

The question which seated itself most insistently in his mind was, why had she come? Was it, after all, merely a matter of curiosity? Was her relationship to Sandy McTrigger such that inquisitiveness alone had brought her to see the man who had saved him? Surely she had not been urged by a sense of gratitude, for in no way had she given expression to that. On his death-bed she had almost made fun of him. And she could not have come as a messenger from McTrigger, or she would have left her message. For the first time he began to doubt that she knew the man at all, in spite of the strange thing that had happened under O'Connor's eyes. But she must know Kedsty. She had made no answer to his half-accusation that she was hiding up at the

Inspector's bungalow. He had used that word—"hiding." It should have had an effect. And she was as beautifully unconscious of it as though she had not heard him, and he knew that she had heard him very distinctly. It was then that she had given him that splendid view of her amazingly long lashes and had countered softly,

"What if you shouldn't die?"

Kent felt himself suddenly aglow with an irresistible appreciation of the genius of her subtlety, and with that appreciation came a thrill of deeper understanding. He believed that he knew why she had left him so suddenly. It was because she had seen herself close to the danger-line. There were things which she did not want him to know or question her about, and his daring intimation that she was hiding in Kedsty's bungalow had warned her. Was it possible that Kedsty himself had sent her for some reason which he could not even guess at? Positively it was not because of McTrigger, the man he had saved. At least she would have thanked him in some way. She would not have appeared quite so adorably cold-blooded, quite so sweetly unconscious of the fact that he was dying. If McTrigger's freedom had meant anything to her, she could not have done less than reveal to him a bit of sympathy. And her greatest compliment, if he excepted the kiss, was that she had called him a splendid liar!

Kent grimaced and drew in a deep breath because of the tightness in his chest. Why was it that every one seemed to disbelieve him? Why was it that even this mysterious girl, whom he had never seen before in his life, politely called him a liar when he insisted that he had killed John Barkley? Was the fact of murder necessarily branded in one's face? If so, he had never observed it. Some of the hardest criminals he had brought in from the down-river country were likable-looking men. There was Horrigan, for instance, who for seven long weeks kept him in good humor with his drollery, though he was bringing him in to be hanged. And there were McTab, and *le Bête Noir*—the Black Beast—a lovable vagabond in spite of his record, and Le Beau, the gentlemanly robber of the wilderness mail, and half a dozen others he could recall without any effort at all. No one called them liars when, like real men, they confessed their crimes when they saw their game was up. To a man they had given up the ghost with their boots on, and Kent respected their memory because of it. And he was dying—and even this stranger girl called him a liar? And no case had ever been more complete than his own. He had gone mercilessly into the condemning detail of it all. It was down in black and white. He had signed it. And still he was disbelieved. It was funny, deuced funny, thought Kent.

Until young Mercer opened the door and came in with his late breakfast, he had forgotten that he had really been hungry when he awakened with

Cardigan's stethoscope at his chest. Mercer had amused him from the first. The pink-faced young Englishman, fresh from the old country, could not conceal in his face and attitude the fact that he was walking in the presence of the gallows whenever he entered the room. He was, as he had confided in Cardigan, "beastly hit up" over the thing. To feed and wash a man who would undoubtedly die, but who would be hanged by the neck until he was dead if he lived, filled him with peculiar and at times conspicuous emotions. It was like attending to a living corpse, if such a thing could be conceived. And Mercer had conceived it. Kent had come to regard him as more or less of a barometer giving away Cardigan's secrets. He had not told Cardigan, but had kept the discovery for his own amusement.

This morning Mercer's face was less pink, and his pale eyes were paler, Kent thought. Also he started to sprinkle sugar on his eggs in place of salt.

Kent laughed and stopped his hand. "You may sugar my eggs when I'm dead, Mercer," he said, "but while I'm alive I want salt on 'em! Do you know, old man, you look bad this morning. Is it because this is my last breakfast?"

"I hope not, sir, I hope not," replied Mercer quickly. "Indeed, I hope you are going to live, sir."

"Thanks!" said Kent dryly. "Where is Cardigan?"

"The Inspector sent a messenger for him, sir. I think he has gone to see him. Are your eggs properly done, sir?"

"Mercer, if you ever worked in a butler's pantry, for the love of heaven forget it now!" exploded Kent, "I want you to tell me something straight out. How long have I got?"

Mercer fidgeted for a moment, and a shade or two more of the red went out of his face. "I can't say, sir. Doctor Cardigan hasn't told me. But I think not very long, sir. Doctor Cardigan is cut up all in rags this morning. And Father Layonne is coming to see you at any moment."

"Much obliged," nodded Kent, calmly beginning his second egg. "And, by the way, what did you think of the young lady?"

"Ripping, positively ripping!" exclaimed Mercer.

"That's the word," agreed Kent. "Ripping. It sounds like the calico counter in a dry-goods store, but means a lot. Don't happen to know where she is staying or why she is at the Landing, do you?"

He knew that he was asking a foolish question and scarcely expected an answer from Mercer. He was astonished when the other said:

"I heard Doctor Cardigan ask her if we might expect her to honor us with another visit, and she told him it would be impossible, because she was leaving on a down-river scow tonight. Fort Simpson, I think she said she was going to, sir."

"The deuce you say!" cried Kent, spilling a bit of his coffee in the thrill of the moment. "Why, that's where Staff-Sergeant O'Connor is bound for!"

"So I heard Doctor Cardigan tell her. But she didn't reply to that. She just— went. If you don't mind a little joke in your present condition, sir, I might say that Doctor Cardigan was considerably flayed up over her. A deuced pretty girl, sir, deuced pretty! And I think he was shot through!"

"Now you're human, Mercer. She was pretty, wasn't she?"

"Er—yes—stunningly so, Mr. Kent," agreed Mercer, reddening suddenly to the roots of his pasty, blond hair. "I don't mind confessing that in this unusual place her appearance was quite upsetting."

"I agree with you, friend Mercer," nodded Kent. "She upset me. And—see here, old man!—will you do a dying man the biggest favor he ever asked in his life?"

"I should be most happy, sir, most happy."

"It's this," said Kent. "I want to know if that girl actually leaves on the down-river scow tonight. If I'm alive tomorrow morning, will you tell me?"

"I shall do my best, sir."

"Good. It's simply the silly whim of a dying man, Mercer. But I want to be humored in it. And I'm sensitive—like yourself. I don't want Cardigan to know. There's an old Indian named Mooie, who lives in a shack just beyond the sawmill. Give him ten dollars and tell him there is another ten in it if he sees the business through, and reports properly to you, and keeps his mouth shut afterward. Here—the money is under my pillow."

Kent pulled out a wallet and put fifty dollars in Mercer's hands.

"Buy cigars with the rest of it, old man. It's of no more use to me. And this little trick you are going to pull off is worth it. It's my last fling on earth, you might say."

"Thank you, sir. It is very kind of you."

Mercer belonged to a class of wandering Englishmen typical of the Canadian West, the sort that sometimes made real Canadians wonder why a big and glorious country like their own should cling to the mother country. Ingratiating and obsequiously polite at all times, he gave one the impression of having had splendid training as a servant, yet had this intimation been made to him, he would have become highly indignant. Kent had learned their ways pretty well. He had met them in all sorts of places, for one of their inexplicable characteristics was the recklessness and apparent lack of judgment with which they located themselves. Mercer, for instance, should have held a petty clerical job of some kind in a city, and here he was acting as nurse in the heart of a wilderness!

After Mercer had gone with the breakfast things and the money, Kent recalled a number of his species. And he knew that under their veneer of apparent servility was a thing of courage and daring which needed only the right kind of incentive to rouse it. And when roused, it was peculiarly efficient in a secretive, artful-dodger sort of way. It would not stand up before a gun. But it would creep under the mouths of guns on a black night. And Kent was positive his fifty dollars would bring him results—if he lived.

Just why he wanted the information he was after, he could not have told himself. It was a pet aphorism between O'Connor and him that they had often traveled to success on the backs of their hunches. And his proposition to Mercer was made on the spur of one of those moments when the spirit of a hunch possessed him. His morning had been one of unexpected excitement, and now he leaned back in an effort to review it and to forget, if he could, the distressing thing that was bound to happen to him within the next few hours. But he could not get away from the thickening in his chest. It seemed growing on him. Now and then he was compelled to make quite an effort to get sufficient air into his lungs.

He found himself wondering if there was a possibility that the girl might return. For a long time he lay thinking about her, and it struck him as incongruous and in bad taste that fate should have left this adventure for his last. If he had met her six months ago—or even three—it was probable that she would so have changed the events of life for him that he would not have got the half-breed's bullet in his chest. He confessed the thing unblushingly. The wilderness had taken the place of woman for him. It had claimed him, body and soul. He had desired nothing beyond its wild freedom and its never-ending games of chance. He had dreamed, as every man dreams, but realities and not the dreams had been the red pulse of his life. And yet, if this girl had come sooner—

He revisioned for himself over and over again her hair and eyes, the slimness of her as she had stood at the window, the freedom and strength of that slender body, the poise of her exquisite head, and he felt again the thrill of her hand and the still more wonderful thrill of her lips as she had pressed them warmly upon his.

And she was of the North! That was the thought that overwhelmed him. He did not permit himself to believe that she might have told him an untruth. He was confident, if he lived until tomorrow, that Mercer would corroborate his faith in her. He had never heard of a place called the Valley of Silent Men, but it was a big country, and Fort Simpson with its Hudson Bay Company's post and its half-dozen shacks was a thousand miles away. He was not sure that such a place as that valley really existed. It was easier to believe that the girl's home was at Fort Providence, Fort Simpson, Fort Good Hope, or even at Fort McPherson. It was not difficult for him to picture her as the daughter of one of the factor lords of the North. Yet this, upon closer consideration, he gave up as unreasonable. The word "Fort" did not stand for population, and there were probably not more than fifty white people at all the posts between the Great Slave and the Arctic. She was not one of these, or the fact would have been known at the Landing.

Neither could she be a riverman's daughter, for it was inconceivable that either a riverman or a trapper would have sent this girl down into civilization, where this girl had undoubtedly been. It was that point chiefly which puzzled Kent. She was not only beautiful. She had been tutored in schools that were not taught by wilderness missioners. In her, it seemed to him, he had seen the beauty and the wild freedom of the forests as they had come to him straight out of the heart of an ancient aristocracy that was born nearly two hundred years ago in the old cities of Quebec and Montreal.

His mind flashed back at that thought: he remembered the time when he had sought out every nook and cranny of that ancient town of Quebec, and had stood over graves two centuries old, and deep in his soul had envied the dead the lives they had lived. He had always thought of Quebec as a rare old bit of time-yellowed lace among cities—the heart of the New World as it had once been, still beating, still whispering of its one-time power, still living in the memory of its mellowed romance, its almost forgotten tragedies—a ghost that lived, that still beat back defiantly the destroying modernism that would desecrate its sacred things. And it pleased him to think of Marette Radisson as the spirit of it, wandering north, and still farther north—even as the spirits of the profaned dead had risen from the Landing to go farther on.

And feeling that the way had at last been made easy for him, Kent smiled out into the glorious day and whispered softly, as if she were standing there, listening to him:

"If I had lived—I would have called you—my Quebec. It's pretty, that name. It stands for a lot. And so do you."

And out in the hall, as Kent whispered those words, stood Father Layonne, with a face that was whiter than the mere presence of death had ever made it before. At his side stood Cardigan, aged ten years since he had placed his stethoscope at Kent's chest that morning. And behind these two were Kedsty, with a face like gray rock, and young Mercer, in whose staring eyes was the horror of a thing he could not yet quite comprehend. Cardigan made an effort to speak and failed. Kedsty wiped his forehead, as he had wiped it the morning of Kent's confession. And Father Layonne, as he went to Kent's door, was breathing softly to himself a prayer.

CHAPTER VII

From the window, the glorious day outside, and the vision he had made for himself of Marette Radisson, Kent turned at the sound of a hand at his door and saw it slowly open. He was expecting it. He had read young Mercer like a book. Mercer's nervousness and the increased tightening of the thing in his chest had given him warning. The thing was going to happen soon, and Father Layonne had come. He tried to smile, that he might greet his wilderness friend cheerfully and unafraid. But the smile froze when the door opened and he saw the missioner standing there.

More than once he had accompanied Father Layonne over the threshold of life into the presence of death, but he had never before seen in his face what he saw there now. He stared. The missioner remained in the doorway, hesitating, as if at the last moment a great fear held him back. For an interval the eyes of the two men rested upon each other in a silence that was like the grip of a living thing. Then Father Layonne came quietly into the room and closed the door behind him.

Kent drew a deep breath and tried to grin. "You woke me out of a dream," he said, "a day-dream. I've had a very pleasant experience this morning, *mon père.*"

"So some one was trying to tell me, Jimmy," replied the little missioner with an effort to smile back.

"Mercer?"

"Yes. He told me about it confidentially. The poor boy must have fallen in love with the young lady."

"So have I, *mon père.* I don't mind confessing it to you. I'm rather glad. And if Cardigan hadn't scheduled me to die—"

"Jimmy," interrupted the missioner quickly, but a bit huskily, "has it ever occurred to you that Doctor Cardigan may be mistaken?"

He had taken one of Kent's hands. His grip tightened. It began to hurt. And Kent, looking into his eyes, found his brain all at once like a black room suddenly illuminated by a flash of fire. Drop by drop the blood went out of his face until it was whiter than Father Layonne's.

"You—you don't—mean—"

"Yes, yes, boy, I mean just that," said the missioner, in a voice so strange that it did not seem to be his own. "You are not going to die, Jimmy. You are going to live!"

"Live!" Kent dropped back against his pillows. "*Live!*" His lips gasped the one word.

He closed his eyes for an instant, and it seemed to him that the world was aflame. And he repeated the word again, but only his lips formed it, and there came no sound. His senses, strained to the breaking-point to meet the ordeal of death, gave way slowly to the mighty reaction. He felt in those moments like a reeling man. He opened his eyes, and there was a meaningless green haze through the window where the world should have been. But he heard Father Layonne's voice. It seemed a great distance off, but it was very clear. Doctor Cardigan had made an error, it was saying. And Doctor Cardigan, because of that error, was like a man whose heart had been taken out of him. But it was an excusable error.

If there had been an X-ray—But there had been none. And Doctor Cardigan had made the diagnosis that nine out of ten good surgeons would probably have made. What he had taken to be the aneurismal blood-rush was an exaggerated heart murmur, and the increased thickening in his chest was a simple complication brought about by too much night air. It was too bad the error had happened. But he must not blame Cardigan!

He must not blame Cardigan! Those last words pounded like an endless series of little waves in Kent's brain. He must not blame Cardigan! He laughed, laughed before his dazed senses readjusted themselves, before the world through the window pieced itself into shape again. At least he thought he was laughing. He must—not—blame—Cardigan! What an amazingly stupid thing for Father Layonne to say! Blame Cardigan for giving him back his life? Blame him for the glorious knowledge that he was not going to die? Blame him for—

Things were coming clearer. Like a bolt slipping into its groove his brain found itself. He saw Father Layonne again, with his white, tense face and eyes in which were still seated the fear and the horror he had seen in the doorway. It was not until then that he gripped fully at the truth.

"I—I see," he said. "You and Cardigan think it would have been better if I had died!"

The missioner was still holding his hand. "I don't know, Jimmy, I don't know. What has happened is terrible."

"But not so terrible as death," cried Kent, suddenly growing rigid against his pillows. "Great God, *mon père*, I want to live! Oh—"

He snatched his hand free and stretched forth both arms to the open window. "Look at it out there! My world again! MY WORLD! I want to go back to it. It's ten times more precious to me now than it was. Why should I blame Cardigan? *Mon père--mon père*--listen to me. I can say it now, because I've got a right to say it. *I lied.* I didn't kill John Barkley!"

A strange cry fell from Father Layonne's lips. It was a choking cry, a cry, not of rejoicing, but of a grief-stung thing. "Jimmy!"

"I swear it! Great heaven, *mon père*, don't you believe me?"

The missioner had risen. In his eyes and face was another look. It was as if in all his life he had never seen James Kent before. It was a look born suddenly of shock, the shock of amazement, of incredulity, of a new kind of horror. Then swiftly again his countenance changed, and he put a hand on Kent's head.

"God forgive you, Jimmy," he said. "And God help you, too!"

Where a moment before Kent had felt the hot throb of an inundating joy, his heart was chilled now by the thing he sensed in Father Layonne's voice and saw in his face and eyes. It was not entirely disbelief. It was a more hopeless thing than that.

"You do not believe me!" he said.

"It is my religion to believe, Jimmy," replied Father Layonne in a gentle voice into which the old calmness had returned. "I must believe, for your sake. But it is not a matter of human sentiment now, lad. It is the Law! Whatever my heart feels toward you can do you no good. You are—" He hesitated to speak the words.

Then it was that Kent saw fully and clearly the whole monstrous situation. It had taken time for it to fasten itself upon him. In a general way it had been clear to him a few moments before; now, detail by detail, it closed in upon him, and his muscles tightened, and Father Layonne saw his jaw set hard and his hands clench. Death was gone. But the mockery of it, the grim exultation of the thing over the colossal trick it had played, seemed to din an infernal laughter in his ears. But—he was going to live! That was the one fact that rose above all others. No matter what happened to him a month or six months from now, he was not going to die today. He would live to receive Mercer's report. He would live to stand on his feet again and to fight for the life which he had thrown away. He was, above everything else, a fighting man. It was born in him to fight, not so much against his fellow men as against the overwhelming odds of adventure as they came to him. And now he was up against the deadliest game of all. He saw it. He felt it. The thing gripped him. In the eyes of that Law of which he had so recently been a part he was a murderer. And in the province of Alberta the penalty for killing a man was hanging. Because horror and fear did not seize upon him, he wondered if he still realized the situation. He believed that he did. It was merely a matter of human nature. Death, he had supposed, was a fixed and foregone thing. He had believed that only a few hours of life were left for him. And now it was given back to him, for months at least. It was a glorious reprieve, and—

Suddenly his heart stood still in the thrill of the thought that came to him. Marette Radisson had known that he was not going to die! She had hinted the fact, and he, like a blundering idiot, had failed to catch the significance of it. She had given him no sympathy, had laughed at him, had almost made fun of him, simply because she knew that he was going to live!

He turned suddenly on Father Layonne.

"They shall believe me!" he cried. "I shall make them believe me! *Mon père*, I lied! I lied to save Sandy McTrigger, and I shall tell them why. If Doctor Cardigan has not made another mistake, I want them all here again. Will you arrange it?"

"Inspector Kedsty is waiting outside," said Father Layonne quietly, "but I should not act in haste, Jimmy. I should wait. I should think—think."

"You mean take time to think up a story that will hold water, *mon père*? I have that. I have the story. And yet—" He smiled a bit dismally. "I did make one pretty thorough confession, didn't I, Father?"

"It was very convincing, Jimmy. It went so particularly into the details, and those details, coupled with the facts that you were seen at John Barkley's earlier in the evening, and that it was you who found him dead a number of hours later—"

"All make a strong case against me," agreed Kent. "As a matter of fact, I was up at Barkley's to look over an old map he had made of the Porcupine country twenty years ago. He couldn't find it. Later he sent word he had run across it. I returned and found him dead."

The little missioner nodded, but did not speak.

"It is embarrassing," Kent went on. "It almost seems as though I ought to go through with it, like a sport. When a man loses, it isn't good taste to set up a howl. It makes him sort of yellow-backed, you know. To play the game according to rules, I suppose I ought to keep quiet and allow myself to be hung without making any disturbance. Die game, and all that, you know. Then there is the other way of looking at it. This poor neck of mine depends on me. It has given me a lot of good service. It has been mighty loyal. It has even swallowed eggs on the day it thought it was going to die. And I'd be a poor specimen of humanity to go back on it now. I want to do that neck a good turn. I want to save it. And I'm going to—if I can!"

In spite of the unpleasant tension of the moment, it cheered Father Layonne to see this old humor returning into the heart of his friend. With him love was an enduring thing. He might grieve for James Kent, he might pray for the salvation of his soul, he might believe him guilty, yet he still bore for him the affection which was too deeply rooted in his heart to be uptorn by physical things or the happenings of chance. So the old cheer of his smile came back, and he said:

"To fight for his life is a privilege which God gives to every man, Jimmy. I was terrified when I came to you. I believed it would have been better if you had died. I can see my error. It will be a terrible fight. If you win, I shall be glad. If you lose, I know that you will lose bravely. Perhaps you are right. It may be best to see Inspector Kedsty before you have had time to think. That point will have its psychological effect. Shall I tell him you are prepared to see him?"

Kent nodded. "Yes. Now."

Father Layonne went to the door. Even there he seemed to hesitate an instant, as if again to call upon Kent to reconsider. Then he opened it and went out.

Kent waited impatiently. His hand, fumbling at his bedclothes, seized upon the cloth with which he had wiped his lips, and it suddenly occurred to him that it had been a long time since it had shown a fresh stain of blood. Now that he knew it was not a deadly thing, the tightening in his chest was less uncomfortable. He felt like getting up and meeting his visitors on his feet. Every nerve in his body wanted action, and the minutes of silence which followed the closing of the door after the missioner were drawn out and tedious to him. A quarter of an hour passed before he heard returning footsteps, and by the sound of them he knew Kedsty was not coming alone. Probably *le pere* would return with him. And possibly Cardigan.

What happened in the next few seconds was somewhat of a shock to him. Father Layonne entered first, and then came Inspector Kedsty. Kent's eyes shot to the face of the commander of N Division. There was scarcely recognition in it. A mere inclination of the head, not enough to call a greeting, was the reply to Kent's nod and salute. Never had he seen Kedsty's face more like the face of an emotionless sphinx. But what disturbed him most was the presence of people he had not expected. Close behind Kedsty was McDougal, the magistrate, and behind McDougal entered Constables Felly and Brant, stiffly erect and clearly under orders. Cardigan, pale and uneasy, came in last, with the stenographer. Scarcely had they entered the room when Constable Pelly pronounced the formal warning of the Criminal Code of the Royal Northwest Mounted Police, and Kent was legally under arrest.

He had not looked for this. He knew, of course, that the process of the Law would take its course, but he had not anticipated this bloodthirsty suddenness. He had expected, first of all, to talk with Kedsty as man to man. And yet—it was the Law. He realized this as his eyes traveled from Kedsty's rock-like face to the expressionless immobility of his old friends, Constables Pelly and Brant. If there was sympathy, it was hidden except in the faces of Cardigan and Father Layonne. And Kent, exultantly hopeful a little while before, felt his heart grow heavy within him as he waited for the moment when he would begin the fight to repossess himself of the life and freed which he had lost.

CHAPTER VIII

For some time after the door to Kent's room had closed upon the ominous visitation of the Law, young Mercer remained standing in the hall, debating with himself whether his own moment had not arrived. In the end he decided that it had, and with Kent's fifty dollars in his pocket he made for the shack of the old Indian trailer, Mooie. It was an hour later when he returned, just in time to see Kent's door open again. Doctor Cardigan and Father Layonne reappeared first, followed in turn by the blonde stenographer, the magistrate, and Constables Pelly and Brant. Then the door closed.

Within the room, sweating from the ordeal through which he had passed, Kent sat bolstered against his pillows, facing Inspector Kedsty with blazing eyes.

"I've asked for these few moments alone with you, Kedsty, because I wanted to talk to you as a man, and not as my superior officer. I am, I take it, no longer a member of the force. That being the case, I owe you no more respect than I owe to any other man. And I am pleased to have the very great privilege of calling you a cursed scoundrel!"

Kedsty's face was hot, but as his hands clenched slowly, it turned redder. Before he could speak, Kent went on.

"You have not shown me the courtesy or the sympathy you have had for the worst criminals that ever faced you. You amazed every man that was in this room, because at one time—if not now—they were my friends. It wasn't what you said. It was how you said it. Whenever there was an inclination on their part to believe, you killed it—not honestly and squarely, by giving me a chance. Whenever you saw a chance for me to win a point, you fell back upon the law. And you don't believe that I killed John Barkley. I know it. You called me a liar the day I made that fool confession. You still believe that I lied. And I have waited until we were alone to ask you certain things, for I still have something of courtesy left in me, if you haven't. What is your game? What has brought about the change in you? Is it—"

His right hand clenched hard as a rock as he leaned toward Kedsty.

"Is it because of the girl hiding up at your bungalow, Kedsty?"

Even in that moment, when he had the desire to strike the man before him, it was impossible for him not to admire the stone-like invulnerability of Kedsty. He had never heard of another man calling Kedsty a scoundrel or dishonest. And yet, except that his faced burned more dully red, the Inspector was as impassively calm as ever. Even Kent's intimation that he was playing a game, and his direct accusation that he was keeping Marette Radisson in hiding at his bungalow, seemed to have no disturbing effect on him. For a space he looked at Kent, as if measuring the poise of the other's mind. When he spoke, it was in a voice so quiet and calm that Kent stared at him in amazement.

"I don't blame you, Kent," he said. "I don't blame you for calling me a scoundrel, or anything else you want to. I think I should do the same if I were in your place. You think it is incredible, because of our previous association, that I should not make every effort to save you. I would, if I thought you were innocent. But I don't. I believe you are guilty. I cannot see where there is a loophole in the evidence against you, as given in your own confession. Why, man, even if I could help to prove you innocent of killing John Barkley—"

He paused and twisted one of his gray mustaches, half facing the window for a moment. "Even if I did that," he went on, "you would still have twenty years of prison ahead of you for the worst kind of perjury on the face of the earth, perjury committed at a time when you thought you were dying! You are guilty, Kent. If not of one thing, then of the other. I am not playing a game. And as for the girl—there is no girl at my bungalow."

He turned to the door; and Kent made no effort to stop him. Words came to his lips and died there, and for a space after Kedsty had gone he stared out into the green forest world beyond his window, seeing nothing. Inspector Kedsty, quietly and calmly, had spoken words that sent his hopes crashing in ruin about him. For even if he escaped the hangman, he was still a criminal— a criminal of the worst sort, perhaps, next to the man who kills another. If he proved that he had not killed John Barkley, he would convict himself, at the same time, of having made solemn oath to a lie on what he supposed was his death-bed. And for that, a possible twenty years in the Edmonton penitentiary! At best he could not expect less than ten. Ten years—twenty years—in prison! That, or hang.

The sweat broke out on his face. He did not curse Kedsty now. His anger was gone. Kedsty had seen all the time what he, like a fool, had not thought of. No matter how the Inspector might feel in that deeply buried heart of his, he could not do otherwise than he was doing. He, James Kent, who hated a lie above all the things on the earth, was kin-as-kisew—the blackest liar of all, a man who lied when he was dying.

And for that lie there was a great punishment. The Law saw with its own eyes. It was a single-track affair, narrow-visioned, caring nothing for what was to the right or the left. It would tolerate no excuse which he might find for himself. He had lied to save a human life, but that life the Law itself had wanted. So he had both robbed and outraged the Law, even though a miracle saved him the greatest penalty of all.

The weight of the thing crushed him. It was as if for the first time a window had opened for him, and he saw what Kedsty had seen. And then, as the minutes passed, the fighting spirit in him rose again. He was not of the sort to go under easily. Personal danger had always stirred him to his greatest depths, and he had never confronted a danger greater than this he was facing now. It was not a matter of leaping quickly and on the spur of the moment. For ten years his training had been that of a hunter of men, and the psychology of the man hunt had been his strong point. Always, in seeking his quarry, he had tried first to bring himself into a mental sympathy and understanding with that quarry. To analyze what an outlaw would do under certain conditions and with certain environments and racial inheritances behind him was to Kent the premier move in the thrilling game. He had evolved rules of great importance for himself, but always he had worked them out from the vantage point of the huntsman. Now he began to turn them around. He, James Kent, was no longer the hunter, but the hunted, and all the tricks which he had mastered must now be worked the other way. His woodcraft, his cunning, the fine points he had learned of the game of one-against-one would avail him but little when it came to the witness chair and a trial.

The open window was his first inspiration. Adventure had been the blood of his life. And out there, behind the green forests rolling away like the billows of an ocean, lay the greatest adventure of all. Once in those beloved forests covering almost the half of a continent, he would be willing to die if the world beat him. He could see himself playing the game of the hunted as no other man had ever played it before. Let him once have his guns and his freedom, with all that world waiting for him—

Eagerness gleamed in his eyes, and then, slowly, it died out. The open window, after all, was but a mockery. He rolled sideways from his bed and partly balanced himself on his feet. The effort made him dizzy. He doubted if he could have walked a hundred yards after climbing through the window. Instantly another thought leaped into his brain. His head was clearing. He swayed across the room and back again, the first time he had been on his feet since the half-breed's bullet had laid him out. He would fool Cardigan. He would fool Kedsty. As he recovered his strength, he would keep it to himself. He would play sick man to the limit, and then some night he would take advantage of the open window!

The thought thrilled him as no other thing in the world had ever thrilled him before. For the first time he sensed the vast difference between the hunter and the hunted, between the man who played the game of life and death alone and the one who played it with the Law and all its might behind him. To hunt was thrilling. To be hunted was more thrilling. Every nerve in his body tingled. A different kind of fire burned in his brain. He was the creature who was at bay. The other fellow was the hunter now.

He went back to the window and leaned far out. He looked at the forest and saw it with new eyes. The gleam of the slowly moving river held a meaning for him that it had never held before. Doctor Cardigan, seeing him then, would have sworn the fever had returned. His eyes held a slumbering fire. His face was flushed. In these moments Kent did not see death. He was not visioning the iron bars of a prison. His blood pulsed only to the stir of that greatest of all adventures which lay ahead of him. He, the best man-hunter in two thousand miles of wilderness, would beat the hunters themselves. The hound had turned fox, and that fox knew the tricks of both the hunter and the hunted. He would win! A world beckoned to him, and he would reach the heart of that world. Already there began to flash through his mind memory of the places where he could find safety and freedom for all time. No man in all the Northland knew its out-of-the-way corners better than he—its unmapped and unexplored places, the far and mysterious patches of *terra incognita*, where the sun still rose and set without permission of the Law, and God laughed as in the days when prehistoric monsters fed from the tops of trees no taller than themselves. Once through that window, with the strength to travel, and the Law might seek him for a hundred years without profit to itself.

It was not bravado in his blood that stirred these thoughts. It was not panic or an unsound excitement. He was measuring things even as he visioned them. He would go down-river way, toward the Arctic. And he would find Marette Radisson! Yes, even though she lived at Barracks at Fort Simpson, he would find her! And after that? The question blurred all other questions in his mind. There were many answers to it.

Knowing that it would be fatal to his scheme if he were found on his feet, he returned to his bed. The flush of his exertion and excitement was still in his face when Doctor Cardigan came half an hour later.

Within the next few minutes he put Cardigan more at his ease than he had been during the preceding day and night. It was, after all, an error which made him happier the more he thought about it, he told the surgeon. He admitted that at first the discovery that he was going to live had horrified him. But now the whole thing bore a different aspect for him. As soon as he was sufficiently strong, he would begin gathering the evidences for his alibi, and he was confident of proving himself innocent of John Barkley's murder.

He anticipated ten years in the Edmonton penitentiary. But what were ten years there as compared with forty or fifty under the sod? He wrung Cardigan's hand. He thanked him for the splendid care he had given him. It was he, Cardigan, who had saved him from the grave, he said—and Cardigan grew younger under his eyes.

"I thought you'd look at it differently, Kent," he said, drawing in a deep breath. "My God, when I found I had made that mistake—"

"You figured you were handing me over to the hangman," smiled Kent. "It's true I shouldn't have made that confession, old man, if I hadn't rated you right next to God Almighty when it came to telling whether a man was going to live or die. But we all make slips. I've made 'em. And you've got no apology to make. I may ask you to send me good cigars now and then while I'm in retirement at Edmonton, and I shall probably insist that you come to smoke with me occasionally and tell me the news of the rivers. But I'm afraid, old chap, that I'm going to worry you a bit more here. I feel queer today, queer inside me. Now it would be a topping joke if some other complication should set in and fool us all again, wouldn't it?"

He could see the impression he was making on Cardigan. Again his faith in the psychology of the mind found its absolute verification. Cardigan, lifted unexpectedly out of the slough of despond by the very man whom he expected to condemn him, became from that moment, in the face of the mental reaction, almost hypersympathetic. When finally he left the room, Kent was inwardly rejoicing. For Cardigan had told him it would be some time before he was strong enough to stand on his feet.

He did not see Mercer all the rest of that day. It was Cardigan who personally brought his dinner and his supper and attended him last at night. He asked not to be interrupted again, as he felt that he wanted to sleep. There was a guard outside his door now.

Cardigan scowled when he volunteered this information. It was sheer nonsense in Kedsty taking such a silly precaution. But he would give the guard rubber-soled shoes and insist that he make no sound that would disturb him. Kent thanked him, and grinned exultantly when he was gone.

He waited until his watch told him it was ten o'clock before he began the exercise which he had prescribed for himself. Noiselessly he rolled out of bed. There was no sensation of dizziness when he stood on his feet this time. His head was as clear as a bell. He began experimenting by inhaling deeper and still deeper breaths and by straightening his chest.

There was no pain, as he had expected there would be. He felt like crying out in his joy. One after the other he stretched up his arms. He bent over until the tips of his fingers touched the floor. He crooked his knees, leaned from side to side, changed from one attitude to another, amazed at the strength and elasticity of his body. Twenty times, before he returned to his bed, he walked back and forth across his room.

He was sleepless. Lying with his back to the pillows he looked out into the starlight, watching for the first glow of the moon and listening again to the owls that had nested in the lightning-shriven tree. An hour later he resumed his exercise.

He was on his feet when through his window he heard the sound of approaching voices and then of running feet. A moment later some one was pounding at a door, and a loud voice shouted for Doctor Cardigan. Kent drew cautiously nearer the window. The moon had risen, and he saw figures approaching, slowly, as if weighted under a burden. Before they turned out of his vision, he made out two men bearing some heavy object between them. Then came the opening of a door, other voices, and after that an interval of quiet.

He returned to his bed, wondering who the new patient could be.

He was breathing easier after his exertion. The fact that he was feeling keenly alive, and that the thickening in his chest was disappearing, flushed him with elation. An unbounded optimism possessed him. It was late when he fell asleep, and he slept late. It was Mercer's entrance into his room that roused him. He came in softly, closed the door softly, yet Kent heard him. The moment he pulled himself up, he knew that Mercer had a report to make, and he also saw that something upsetting had happened to him. Mercer was a bit excited.

"I beg pardon for waking you, sir," he said, leaning close over Kent, as though fearing the guard might be listening at the door. "But I thought it best for you to hear about the Indian, sir."

"The Indian?"

"Yes, sir—Mooie, sir. I am quite upset over it, Mr. Kent. He told me early last evening that he had found the scow on which the girl was going down-river. He said it was hidden in Kim's Bayou."

"Kim's Bayou! That was a good hiding-place, Mercer!"

"A very good place of concealment indeed, sir. As soon as it was dark, Mooie returned to watch. What happened to him I haven't fully discovered, sir. But it must have been near midnight when he staggered up to Crossen's place, bleeding and half out of his senses. They brought him here, and I watched over him most of the night. He says the girl went aboard the scow and that the scow started down-river. That much I learned, sir. But all the rest he mumbles in a tongue I can not understand. Crossen says it's Cree, and that old Mooie believes devils jumped on him with clubs down at Kim's Bayou. Of course they must have been men. I don't believe in Mooie's devils, sir."

"Nor I," said Kent, the blood stirring strangely in his veins. "Mercer, it simply means there was some one cleverer than old Mooie watching that trail."

With a curiously tense face Mercer was looking cautiously toward the door. Then he leaned still lower over Kent.

"During his mumblings, when I was alone with him, I heard him speak a name, sir. Half a dozen times, sir—and it was—*Kedsty*!"

Kent's fingers gripped the young Englishman's hand.

"You heard *that*, Mercer?"

"I am sure I could not have been mistaken, sir. It was repeated a number of times."

Kent fell back against his pillows. His mind was working swiftly. He knew that behind an effort to appear calm Mercer was uneasy over what had happened.

"We mustn't let this get out, Mercer," he said. "If Mooie should be badly hurt—should die, for instance—and it was discovered that you and I—"

He knew he had gone far enough to give effect to his words. He did not even look at Mercer.

"Watch him closely, old man, and report to me everything that happens. Find out more about Kedsty, if you can. I shall advise you how to act. It is rather ticklish, you know—for you! And"—he smiled at Mercer—"I'm unusually hungry this morning. Add another egg, will you, Mercer? Three instead of two, and a couple of extra slices of toast. And don't let any one know that my appetite is improving. It may be best for both of us—especially if Mooie should happen to die. Understand, old man?"

"I—I think I do, sir," replied Mercer, paling at the grimly smiling thing he saw in Kent's eyes. "I shall do as you say, sir."

When he had gone, Kent knew that he had accurately measured his man. True to a certain type, Mercer would do a great deal for fifty dollars—under cover. In the open he was a coward. And Kent knew the value of such a man under certain conditions. The present was one of those conditions. From this hour Mercer would be a priceless asset to his scheme for personal salvation.

CHAPTER IX

That morning Kent ate a breakfast that would have amazed Doctor Cardigan and would have roused a greater caution in Inspector Kedsty had he known of it. While eating he strengthened the bonds already welded between himself and Mercer. He feigned great uneasiness over the condition of Mooie, who he knew was not fatally hurt because Mercer had told him there was no fracture. But if he should happen to die, he told Mercer, it would mean something pretty bad for them, if their part in the affair leaked out.

As for himself, it would make little difference, as he was "in bad" anyway. But he did not want to see a good friend get into trouble on his account. Mercer was impressed. He saw himself an instrument in a possible murder affair, and the thought terrified him. Even at best, Kent told him, they had given and taken bribes, a fact that would go hard with them unless Mooie kept his mouth shut. And if the Indian knew anything out of the way about Kedsty, it was mighty important that he, Mercer, get hold of it, for it might prove a trump card with them in the event of a showdown with the Inspector of Police. As a matter of form, Mercer took his temperature. It was perfectly normal, but it was easy for Kent to persuade a notation on the chart a degree above.

"Better keep them thinking I'm still pretty sick," he assured Mercer. "They won't suspect there is anything between us then."

Mercer was so much in sympathy with the idea that he suggested adding another half-degree.

It was a splendid day for Kent. He could feel himself growing stronger with each hour that passed. Yet not once during the day did he get out of his bed, fearing that he might be discovered. Cardigan visited him twice and had no suspicion of Mercer's temperature chart. He dressed his wound, which was healing fast. It was the fever which depressed him. There must be, he said, some internal disarrangement which would soon clear itself up. Otherwise there seemed to be no very great reason why Kent should not get on his feet. He smiled apologetically.

"Seems queer to say that, when a little while ago I was telling you it was time to die," he said.

That night, after ten o'clock, Kent went through his setting-up exercises four times. He marveled even more than the preceding night at the swiftness with which his strength was returning. Half a dozen times the little devils of eagerness working in his blood prompted him to take to the window at once.

For three days and nights thereafter he kept his secret and added to his strength. Doctor Cardigan came in to see him at intervals, and Father

Layonne visited him regularly every afternoon. Mercer was his most frequent visitor. On the third day two things happened to create a little excitement. Doctor Cardigan left on a four-day journey to a settlement fifty miles south, leaving Mercer in charge—and Mooie came suddenly out of his fever into his normal senses again. The first event filled Kent with joy. With Cardigan out of the way there would be no immediate danger of the discovery that he was no longer a sick man. But it was the recovery of Mooie from the thumping he had received about the head that delighted Mercer. He was exultant. With the quick reaction of his kind he gloated over the fact before Kent. He let it be known that he was no longer afraid, and from the moment Mooie was out of danger his attitude was such that more than once Kent would have taken keen pleasure in kicking him from the room. Also, from the hour he was safely in charge of Doctor Cardigan's place, Mercer began to swell with importance. Kent saw the new danger and began to humor him. He flattered him. He assured him that it was a burning shame Cardigan had not taken him into partnership. He deserved it. And, in justice to himself, Mercer should demand that partnership when Cardigan returned. He, Kent, would talk to Father Layonne about it, and the missioner would spread the gospel of what ought to be among others who were influential at the Landing. For two days he played with Mercer as an angler plays with a treacherous fish. He tried to get Mercer to discover more about Mooie's reference to Kedsty. But the old Indian had shut up like a clam.

"He was frightened when I told him he had said things about the Inspector," Mercer reported. "He disavowed everything. He shook his head—no, no, no. He had not seen Kedsty. He knew nothing about him. I can do nothing with him, Kent."

He had dropped his "sirs," also his servant-like servility. He helped to smoke Kent's cigars with the intimacy of proprietorship, and with offensive freedom called him "Kent." He spoke of the Inspector as "Kedsty," and of Father Layonne as "the little preacher." He swelled perceptibly, and Kent knew that each hour of that swelling added to his own danger.

He believed that Mercer was talking. Several times a day he heard him in conversation with the guard, and not infrequently Mercer went down to the Landing, twirling a little reed cane that he had not dared to use before. He began to drop opinions and information to Kent in a superior sort of way. On the fourth day word came that Doctor Cardigan would not return for another forty-eight hours, and with unblushing conceit Mercer intimated that when he did return he would find big changes. Then it was that in the stupidity of his egotism he said:

"Kedsty has taken a great fancy to me, Kent. He's a square old top, when you take him right. Had me over this afternoon, and we smoked a cigar together.

When I told him that I looked in at your window last night and saw you going through a lot of exercises, he jumped up as if some one had stuck a pin in him. 'Why, I thought he was sick—*bad*!' he said. And I let him know there were better ways of making a sick man well than Cardigan's. 'Give them plenty to eat,' I said. 'Let 'em live normal,' I argued. 'Look at Kent, for instance,' I told him. 'He's been eating like a bear for a week, and he can turn somersaults this minute!' That topped him over, Kent. I knew it would be a bit of a surprise for him, that I should do what Cardigan couldn't do. He walked back and forth, black as a hat—thinking of Cardigan, I suppose. Then he called in that Pelly chap and gave him something which he wrote on a piece of paper. After that he shook hands with me, slapped me on the shoulder most intimately, and gave me another cigar. He's a keen old blade, Kent. He doesn't need more than one pair of eyes to see what I've done since Cardigan went away!"

If ever Kent's hands had itched to get at the throat of a human being, the yearning convulsed his fingers now. At the moment when he was about to act Mercer had betrayed him to Kedsty! He turned his face away so that Mercer could not see what was in his eyes. Under his body he concealed his clenched hands. Within himself he fought against the insane desire that was raging in his blood, the desire to leap on Mercer and kill him. If Cardigan had reported his condition to Kedsty, it would have been different. He would have accepted the report as a matter of honorable necessity on Cardigan's part. But Mercer—a toad blown up by his own wind, a consummate fiend who would sell his best friend, a fool, an ass—

For a space he held himself rigid as a stone, his face turned away from Mercer. His better sense won. He knew that his last chance depended upon his coolness now. And Mercer unwittingly helped him to win by slyly pocketing a couple of his cigars and leaving the room. For a minute or two Kent heard him talking to the guard outside the door.

He sat up then. It was five o'clock. How long ago was it that Mercer had seen Kedsty? What was the order that the Inspector had written on a sheet of paper for Constable Pelly? Was it simply that he should be more closely watched, or was it a command to move him to one of the cells close to the detachment office? If it was the latter, all his hopes and plans were destroyed. His mind flew to those cells.

The Landing had no jail, not even a guard-house, though the members of the force sometimes spoke of the cells just behind Inspector Kedsty's office by that name. The cells were of cement, and Kent himself had helped to plan them! The irony of the thing did not strike him just then. He was recalling the fact that no prisoner had ever escaped from those cement cells. If no action were taken before six o'clock, he was sure that it would be postponed until the following morning. It was possible that Kedsty's order was for Pelly to prepare a cell for him. Deep in his soul he prayed fervently that it was only a matter of preparation. If they would give him one more night—just one!

His watch tinkled the half-hour. Then a quarter of six. Then six. His blood ran feverishly, in spite of the fact that he possessed the reputation of being the coolest man in N Division. He lighted his last cigar and smoked it slowly to cover the suspense which he feared revealed itself in his face, should any one come into his room. His supper was due at seven. At eight it would begin to get dusk. The moon was rising later each night, and it would not appear over the forests until after eleven. He would go through his window at ten o'clock. His mind worked swiftly and surely as to the method of his first night's flight. There were always a number of boats down at Crossen's place. He would start in one of these, and by the time Mercer discovered he was gone, he would be forty miles on his way to freedom. Then he would set his boat adrift, or hide it, and start cross-country until his trail was lost. Somewhere and in some way he would find both guns and food. It was fortunate that he had not given Mercer the other fifty dollars under his pillow.

At seven Mercer came with his supper. A little gleam of disappointment shot into his pale eyes when he found the last cigar gone from the box. Kent saw the expression and tried to grin good-humoredly.

"I'm going to have Father Layonne bring me up another box in the morning, Mercer," he said. "That is, if I can get hold of him."

"You probably can," snapped Mercer. "He doesn't live far from barracks, and that's where you are going. I've got orders to have you ready to move in the morning."

Kent's blood seemed for an instant to flash into living flame. He drank a part of his cup of coffee and said then, with a shrug of his shoulders: "I'm glad of it, Mercer. I'm anxious to have the thing over. The sooner they get me down there, the quicker they will take action. And I'm not afraid, not a bit of it. I'm bound to win. There isn't a chance in a hundred that they can convict me." Then he added: "And I'm going to have a box of cigars sent up to you, Mercer. I'm grateful to you for the splendid treatment you have given me."

No sooner had Mercer gone with the supper things than Kent's knotted fist shook itself fiercely in the direction of the door.

"My God, how I'd like to have you out in the woods—alone—for just one hour!" he whispered.

Eight o'clock came, and nine. Two or three times he heard voices in the hall, probably Mercer talking with the guard. Once he thought he heard a rumble of thunder, and his heart throbbed joyously. Never had he welcomed a storm as he would have welcomed it tonight. But the skies remained clear. Not only that, but the stars as they began to appear seemed to him more brilliant than he had ever seen them before. And it was very still. The rattle of a scow-chain came up to him from the river as though it were only a hundred yards away. He knew that it was one of Mooie's dogs he heard howling over near the sawmill. The owls, flitting past his window, seemed to click their beaks more loudly than last night. A dozen times he fancied he could hear the rippling voice of the river that very soon was to carry him on toward freedom.

The river! Every dream and aspiration found its voice for him in that river now. Down it Marette Radisson had gone. And somewhere along it, or on the river beyond, or the third river still beyond that, he would find her. In the long, tense wait between the hours of nine and ten he brought the girl back into his room again. He recalled every gesture she had made, every word she had spoken. He felt the thrill of her hand on his forehead, her kiss, and in his brain her softly spoken words repeated themselves over and over again, "I think that if you lived very long I should love you." And as she had spoken those words *she knew that he was not going to die*!

Why, then, had she gone away? Knowing that he was going to live, why had she not remained to help him if she could? Either she had spoken the words in jest, or—

A new thought flashed into his mind. It almost drew a cry from his lips. It brought him up tense, erect, his heart pounding. Had she gone away? Was it not possible that she, too, was playing a game in giving the impression that she was leaving down-river on the hidden scow? Was it conceivable that she was playing that game against Kedsty? A picture, clean-cut as the stars in the sky, began to outline itself in his mental vision. It was clear, now, what Mooie's mumblings about Kedsty had signified. Kedsty had accompanied Marette to the scow. Mooie had seen him and had given the fact away in his fever. Afterward he had clamped his mouth shut through fear of the "big man" of the Law. But why, still later, had he almost been done to death? Mooie was a harmless creature. He had no enemies.

There was no one at the Landing who would have assaulted the old trailer, whose hair was white with age. No one, unless it was Kedsty himself— Kedsty at bay, Kedsty in a rage. Even that was inconceivable. Whatever the motive of the assault might be, and no matter who had committed it, Mooie had most certainly seen the Inspector of Police accompany Marette Radisson to the scow. And the question which Kent found it impossible to answer was, had Marette Radisson really gone down the river on that scow?

It was almost with a feeling of disappointment that he told himself it was possible she had not. He wanted her on the river. He wanted her going north and still farther north. The thought that she was mixed up in some affair that had to do with Kedsty was displeasing to him. If she was still in the Landing or near the Landing, it could no longer be on account of Sandy McTrigger, the man his confession had saved. In his heart he prayed that she was many days down the Athabasca, for it was there—and only there—that he would ever see her again. And his greatest desire, next to his desire for his freedom, was to find her. He was frank with himself in making that confession. He was more than that. He knew that not a day or night would pass that he would not think or dream of Marette Radisson. The wonder of her had grown more vivid for him with each hour that passed, and he was sorry now that he had not dared to touch her hair. She would not have been offended with him, for she had kissed him—after he had killed the impulse to lay his hand on that soft glory that had crowned her head.

And then the little bell in his watch tinkled the hour of ten! He sat up with a jerk. For a space he held his breath while he listened. In the hall outside his room there was no sound. An inch at a time he drew himself off his bed until he stood on his feet. His clothes hung on hooks in the wall, and he groped his way to them so quietly that one listening at the crack of his door would not have heard him. He dressed swiftly. Then he made his way to the window, looked out, and listened.

In the brilliant starlight he saw nothing but the two white stubs of the lightning-shattered trees in which the owls lived. And it was very still. The air was fresh and sweet in his face. In it he caught the scent of the distant balsams and cedars. The world, wonderful in its night silence, waited for him. It was impossible for him to conceive of failure or death out there, and it seemed unreal and trivial that the Law should expect to hold him, with that world reaching out its arms to him and calling him.

Assured that the moment for action was at hand, he moved quickly. In another ten seconds he was through the window, and his feet were on the ground. For a space he stood out clear in the starlight. Then he hurried to the end of the building and hid himself in the shadow. The swiftness of his movement had brought him no physical discomfort, and his blood danced with the thrill of the earth under his feet and the thought that his wound must be even more completely healed than he had supposed. A wild exultation swept over him. He was free! He could see the river now, shimmering and talking to him in the starlight, urging him to hurry, telling him that only a little while ago another had gone north on the breast of it, and that if he hastened it would help him to overtake her. He felt the throb of new life in his body. His eyes shone strangely in the semi-gloom.

It seemed to him that only yesterday Marette had gone. She could not be far away, even now. And in these moments, with the breath of freedom stirring him with the glory of new life, she was different for him from what she had ever been. She was a part of him. He could not think of escape without thinking of her. She became, in these precious moments, the living soul of his wilderness. He felt her presence. The thought possessed him that somewhere down the river she was thinking of him, waiting, expecting him. And in that same flash he made up his mind that he would not discard the boat, as he had planned; he would conceal himself by day, and float downstream by night, until at last he came to Marette Radisson. And then he would tell her why he had come. And after that—

He looked toward Crossen's place. He would make straight for it, openly, like a man bent on a mission there was no reason to conceal. If luck went right, and Crossen was abed, he would be on the river within fifteen minutes. His blood ran faster as he took his first step out into the open starlight. Fifty yards ahead of him was the building which Cardigan used for his fuel. Safely beyond that, no one could see him from the windows of the hospital. He walked swiftly. Twenty paces, thirty, forty—and he stopped as suddenly as the half-breed's bullet had stopped him weeks before. Round the end of Cardigan's fuel house came a figure. It was Mercer. He was twirling his little cane and traveling quietly as a cat. They were not ten feet apart, yet Kent had not heard him.

Mercer stopped. The cane dropped from his hand. Even in the starlight Kent could see his face turn white.

"Don't make a sound, Mercer," he warned. "I'm taking a little exercise in the open air. If you cry out, I'll kill you!"

He advanced slowly, speaking in a voice that could not have been heard at the windows behind him. And then a thing happened that froze the blood in his veins. He had heard the scream of every beast of the great forests, but never a scream like that which came from Mercer's lips now. It was not the cry of a man. To Kent it was the voice of a fiend, a devil. It did not call for help. It was wordless. And as the horrible sound issued from Mercer's mouth he could see the swelling throat and bulging eyes that accompanied the effort. They made him think of a snake, a cobra.

The chill went out of his blood, replaced by a flame of hottest fire. He forgot everything but that this serpent was in his path. Twice he had stood in his way. And he hated him. He hated him with a virulency that was death. Neither the call of freedom nor the threat of prison could keep him from wreaking vengeance now. Without a sound he was at Mercer's throat, and the scream ended in a choking shriek. His fingers dug into flabby flesh, and his clenched fist beat again and again into Mercer's face.

He went to the ground, crushing the human serpent under him. And he continued to strike and choke as he had never struck or choked another man, all other things overwhelmed by his mad desire to tear into pieces this two-legged English vermin who was too foul to exist on the face of the earth.

And he still continued to strike—even after the path lay clear once more between him and the river.

CHAPTER X

What a terrible and inexcusable madness had possessed him, Kent realized the instant he rose from Mercer's prostrate body. Never had his brain flamed to that madness before. He believed at first that he had killed Mercer. It was neither pity nor regret that brought him to his senses. Mercer, a coward and a traitor, a sneak of the lowest type, had no excuse for living. It was the thought that he had lost his chance to reach the river that cleared his head as he swayed over Mercer.

He heard running feet. He saw figures approaching swiftly through the starlight. And he was too weak to fight or run. The little strength he had saved up, and which he had planned to use so carefully in his flight, was gone. His wound, weeks in bed, muscles unaccustomed to the terrific exertion he had made in these moments of his vengeance, left him now panting and swaying as the running footsteps came nearer.

His head swam. For a space he was sickeningly dizzy, and in the first moment of that dizziness, when every drop of blood in his body seemed rushing to his brain, his vision was twisted and his sense of direction gone. In his rage he had overexerted himself. He knew that something had gone wrong inside him and that he was helpless. Even then his impulse was to stagger toward the inanimate Mercer and kick him, but hands caught him and held him. He heard an amazed voice, then another—and something hard and cold shut round his wrists like a pair of toothless jaws.

It was Constable Carter, Inspector Kedsty's right-hand man about barracks, that he saw first; then old Sands, the caretaker at Cardigan's place. Swiftly as he had turned sick, his brain grew clear, and his blood distributed itself evenly again through his body. He held up his hands. Carter had slipped a pair of irons on him, and the starlight glinted on the shining steel. Sands was bending over Mercer, and Carter was saying in a low voice:

"It's too bad, Kent. But I've got to do it. I saw you from the window just as Mercer screamed. Why did you stop for *him*?"

Mercer was getting up with the assistance of Sands. He turned a bloated and unseeing face toward Kent and Carter. He was blubbering and moaning, as though entreating for mercy in the fear that Kent had not finished with him. Carter pulled Kent away.

"There's only one thing for me to do now," he said. "It isn't pleasant. But the law says I must take you to barracks."

In the sky Kent saw the stars clearly again, and his lungs were drinking in the cool air as in the wonderful moments before his encounter with Mercer.

He had lost. And it was Mercer who had made him lose. Carter felt the sudden tightening of his muscles as he walked with a hand on his arm. And Kent shut his teeth close and made no answer to what Carter had said, except that Carter heard something which he thought was a sob choked to death in the other's throat.

Carter, too, was a man bred of the red blood of the North, and he knew what was in Kent's heart. For only by the breadth of a hair had Kent failed in his flight.

Pelly was on duty at barracks, and it was Pelly who locked him in one of the three cells behind the detachment office. When he was gone, Kent sat down on the edge of his prison cot and for the first time let the agony of his despair escape in a gasping breath from between his lips. Half an hour ago the world had reached out its arms to him, and he had gone forth to its welcome, only to have the grimmest tragedy of all his life descend upon him like the sword of Damocles. For this was real tragedy. Here there was no hope. The tentacles of the law had him in their grip, and he could no longer dream of escape.

Ghastly was the thought that it was he, James Kent, who had supervised the building of these cells! Acquainted with every trick and stratagem of the prisoner plotting for his freedom, he had left no weak point in their structure. Again he clenched his hands, and in his soul he cursed Mercer as he went to the little barred window that overlooked the river from his cell. The river was near now. He could hear the murmur of it. He could see its movement, and that movement, played upon by the stars, seemed now a writhing sort of almost noiseless laughter taunting him in his folly.

He went back to his cot, and in his despair buried his face in his hands. In the half-hour after that he did not raise his head. For the first time in his life he knew that he was beaten, so utterly beaten that he no more had the desire to fight, and his soul was dark with the chaos of the things he had lost.

At last he opened his eyes to the blackness of his prison room, and he beheld a marvelous thing. Across the gloom of the cell lay a shaft of golden fire. It was the light of the rising moon coming through his little, steel-barred window. To Kent it had crept into his cell like a living thing. He watched it, fascinated. His eyes followed it to the foot-square aperture, and there, red and glorious as it rose over the forests, the moon itself filled the world. For a space he saw nothing but that moon crowding the frame of his window. And as he rose to his feet and stood where his face was flooded in the light of it, he felt stirring within him the ghosts of his old hopes. One by one they rose up and came to life. He held out his hands, as if to fill them with the liquid glow; his heart beat faster in that glory of the moonrise. The taunting murmur of the river changed once more into hopeful song, his fingers closed tightly around the bars, and the fighting spirit rose in him again. As that spirit surged stronger, beating down his despair, driving the chaos out of his brain, he watched the moon as it climbed higher, changing from the red of the lower atmosphere to the yellow gold of the greater heights, marveling at the miracle of light and color that had never failed to stir him.

And then he laughed. If Pelly or Carter had heard him, they would have wondered if he was mad. It was madness of a sort—the madness of restored confidence, of an unlimited faith, of an optimism that was bound to make dreams come true. Again he looked beyond the bars of his cell. The world was still there; the river was there; all the things that were worth fighting for were there. And he would fight. Just how, he did not try to tell himself now. And then he laughed again, softly, a bit grimly, for he saw the melancholy humour of the fact that he had built his own prison.

He sat down again on the edge of his cot, and the whimsical thought struck him that all those he had brought to this same cell, and who had paid the first of their penance here, must be laughing at him now in the spirit way. In his mental fancy a little army of faces trooped before him, faces dark and white, faces filled with hatred and despair, faces brave with the cheer of hope and faces pallid with the dread of death. And of these ghosts of his man-hunting prowess it was Anton Fournet's face that came out of the crowd and remained with him. For he had brought Anton to this same cell—Anton, the big Frenchman, with his black hair, his black beard, and his great, rolling laugh that even in the days when he was waiting for death had rattled the paper-weights on Kedsty's desk.

Anton rose up like a god before Kent now. He had killed a man, and like a brave man he had not denied it. With a heart in his great body as gentle as a girl's, Anton had taken pride in the killing. In his prison days he sang songs to glorify it. He had killed the white man from Chippewyan who had stolen his neighbor's wife! Not *his* wife, but his neighbor's! For Anton's creed was, "Do unto others as you would have others do unto you," and he had loved his neighbor with the great forest love of man for man. His neighbor was weak, and Anton was strong with the strength of a bull, so that when the hour came, it was Anton who had measured out vengeance. When Kent brought Anton in, the giant had laughed first at the littleness of his cell, then at the unsuspected strength of it, and after that he had laughed and sung great, roaring songs every day of the brief tenure of life that was given him. When he died, it was with the smiling glory in his face of one who had cheaply righted a great wrong.

Kent would never forget Anton Fournet. He had never ceased to grieve that it had been his misfortune to bring Anton in, and always, in close moments, the thought of Anton, the stout-hearted, rallied him back to courage. Never would he be the man that Anton Fournet had been, he told himself many times. Never would his heart be as great or as big, though the Law had hanged Anton by the neck until the soul was choked out of his splendid body, for it was history that Anton Fournet had never harmed man, woman, or child until he set out to kill a human snake and the Law placed its heel upon him and crushed him.

And tonight Anton Fournet came into the cell again and sat with Kent on the cot where he had slept many nights, and the ghosts of his laughter and his song filled Kent's ears, and his great courage poured itself out in the moonlit prison room so that at last, when Kent stretched himself on the cot to sleep, it was with the knowledge that the soul of the splendid dead had given him a strength which it was impossible to have gained from the living. For Anton Fournet had died smiling, laughing, singing—and it was of Anton Fournet that he dreamed when he fell asleep. And in that dream came also the vision of a man called Dirty Fingers—and with it inspiration.

CHAPTER XI

Where a bit of the big river curved inward like the tongue of a friendly dog, lapping the shore at Athabasca Landing, there still remained Fingers' Row— nine dilapidated, weather-worn, and crazily-built shacks put there by the eccentric genius who had foreseen a boom ten years ahead of its time. And the fifth of these nine, counting from either one end or the other, was named by its owner, Dirty Fingers himself, the Good Old Queen Bess. It was a shack covered with black tar paper, with two windows, like square eyes, fronting the river as if always on the watch for something. Across the front of this shack Dirty Fingers had built a porch to protect himself from the rain in springtime, from the sun in Summer time, and from the snow in the months of Winter. For it was here that Dirty Fingers sat out all of that part of his life which was not spent in bed.

Up and down two thousand miles of the Three Rivers was Dirty Fingers known, and there were superstitious ones who believed that little gods and devils came to sit and commune with him in the front of the tar-papered shack. No one was so wise along those rivers, no one was so satisfied with himself, that he would not have given much to possess the many things that were hidden away in Dirty Fingers' brain. One would not have suspected the workings of that brain by a look at Dirty Fingers on the porch of his Good Old Queen Bess. He was a great soft lump of a man, a giant of flabbiness. Sitting in his smooth-worn, wooden armchair, he was almost formless. His head was huge, his hair uncut and scraggy, his face smooth as a baby's, fat as a cherub's, and as expressionless as an apple. His folded arms always rested on a huge stomach, whose conspicuousness was increased by an enormous watch-chain made from beaten nuggets of Klondike gold, and Dirty Fingers' thumb and forefinger were always twiddling at this chain. How he had come by the name of Dirty Fingers, when his right name was Alexander Toppet Fingers, no one could definitely say, unless it was that he always bore an unkempt and unwashed appearance.

Whatever the quality of the two hundred and forty-odd pounds of flesh in Dirty Fingers' body, it was the quality of his brain that made people hold him in a sort of awe. For Dirty Fingers was a lawyer, a wilderness lawyer, a forest bencher, a legal strategist of the trail, of the river, of the great timber-lands.

Stored away in his brain was every rule of equity and common law of the great North country. For his knowledge he went back two hundred years. He knew that a law did not die of age, that it must be legislated to death, and out of the moldering past he had dug up every trick and trap of his trade. He had no law-books. His library was in his head, and his facts were marshaled in pile after pile of closely-written, dust-covered papers in his shack. He did not

•

go to court as other lawyers; and there were barristers in Edmonton who blessed him for that.

His shack was his tabernacle of justice. There he sat, hands folded, and gave out his decisions, his advice, his sentences. He sat until other men would have gone mad. From morning until night, moving only for his meals or to get out of heat or storm, he was a fixture on the porch of the Good Old Queen Bess. For hours he would stare at the river, his pale eyes never seeming to blink. For hours he would remain without a move or a word. One constant companion he had, a dog, fat, emotionless, lazy, like his master. Always this dog was sleeping at his feet or dragging himself wearily at his heels when Dirty Fingers elected to make a journey to the little store where he bartered for food and necessities.

It was Father Layonne who came first to see Kent in his cell the morning after Kent's unsuccessful attempt at flight. An hour later it was Father Layonne who traveled the beaten path to the door of Dirty Fingers' shack. If a visible emotion of pleasure ever entered into Dirty Fingers' face, it was when the little missioner came occasionally to see him. It was then that his tongue let itself loose, and until late at night they talked of many things of which other men knew but little. This morning Father Layonne did not come casually, but determinedly on business, and when Dirty Fingers learned what that business was, he shook his head disconsolately, folded his fat arms more tightly over his stomach, and stated the sheer impossibility of his going to see Kent. It was not his custom. People must come to him. And he did not like to walk. It was fully a third of a mile from his shack to barracks, possibly half a mile. And it was mostly upgrade! If Kent could be brought to him—

In his cell Kent waited. It was not difficult for him to hear voices in Kedsty's office when the door was open, and he knew that the Inspector did not come in until after the missioner had gone on his mission to Dirty Fingers. Usually he was at the barracks an hour or so earlier. Kent made no effort to figure out a reason for Kedsty's lateness, but he did observe that after his arrival there was more than the usual movement between the office door and the outside of the barracks. Once he was positive that he heard Cardigan's voice, and then he was equally sure that he heard Mercer's. He grinned at that. He must be wrong, for Mercer would be in no condition to talk for several days. He was glad that a turn in the hall hid the door of the detachment office from him, and that the three cells were in an alcove, safely out of sight of the curious eyes of visitors. He was also glad that he had no other prisoner for company. His situation was one in which he wanted to be alone. To the plan that was forming itself in his mind, solitude was as vital as the cooperation of Alexander Toppet Fingers.

Just how far he could win that cooperation was the problem which confronted him now, and he waited anxiously for the return of Father Layonne, listening for the sound of his footsteps in the outer hall. If, after all, that inspirational thought of last night came to nothing, if Fingers should fail him—

He shrugged his shoulders. If that happened, he could see no other chance. He would have to go on and take his medicine at the hands of a jury. But if Fingers played up to the game—

He looked out on the river again, and again it was the river that seemed to answer him. If Fingers played with him, they would beat Kedsty and the whole of N Division! And in winning he would prove out the greatest psychological experiment he had ever dared to make. The magnitude of the thing, when he stopped to think of it, was a little appalling, but his faith was equally large. He did not consider his philosophy at all supernatural. He had brought it down to the level of the average man and woman.

He believed that every man and woman possessed a subliminal consciousness which it was possible to rouse to tremendous heights if the right psychological key was found to fit its particular lock, and he believed he possessed the key which fitted the deeply-buried and long-hidden thing in Dirty Fingers' remarkable brain. Because he believed in this metaphysics which he had not read out of Aristotle, he had faith that Fingers would prove his salvation. He felt growing in him stronger than ever a strange kind of elation. He felt better physically than last night. The few minutes of strenuous action in which he had half killed Mercer had been a pretty good test, he told himself. It had left no bad effect, and he need no longer fear the reopening of his wound.

A dozen times he had heard a far door open and close. Now he heard it again, and a few moments later it was followed by a sound which drew a low cry of satisfaction from him. Dirty Fingers, because of overweight and lack of exercise, had what he called an "asthmatic wind," and it was this strenuous working of his lungs that announced his approach to Kent. His dog was also afflicted and for the same reasons, so that when they traveled together there was some rivalry between them.

"We're both bad put out for wind, thank God," Dirty Fingers would say sometimes. "It's a good thing, for if we had more of it, we'd walk farther, and we don't like walking."

The dog was with Fingers now, also Father Layonne, and Pelly. Pelly unlocked the cell, then relocked it again after Fingers and the dog entered. With a nod and a hopeful look the missioner returned with Pelly to the detachment office. Fingers wiped his red face with a big handkerchief, gasping deeply for breath. Togs, his dog, was panting as if he had just finished the race of his life.

"A difficult climb," wheezed Fingers. "A most difficult climb."

He sat down, rolling out like a great bag of jelly in the one chair in the cell, and began to fan himself with his hat. Kent had already taken stock of the situation. In Fingers' florid countenance and in his almost colorless eyes he detected a bit of excitement which Fingers was trying to hide. Kent knew what it meant. Father Layonne had found it necessary to play his full hand to lure Fingers up the hill, and had given him a hint of what it was that Kent had in store for him. Already the psychological key had begun to work.

Kent sat down on the edge of his cot and grinned sympathetically. "It hasn't always been like this, has it, Fingers?" he said then, leaning a bit forward and speaking with a sudden, low-voiced seriousness. "There was a time, twenty years ago, when you didn't puff after climbing a hill. Twenty years make a big difference, sometimes."

"Yes, sometimes," agreed Fingers in a wheezy whisper.

"Twenty years ago you were—a fighter."

It seemed to Kent that a deeper color came into Dirty Fingers' pale eyes in the few seconds that followed these words.

"A fighter," he repeated. "Most men were fighters in those days of the gold rushes, weren't they, Fingers? I've heard a lot of the old stories about them in my wanderings, and some of them have made me thrill. They weren't afraid to die. And most of them were pretty white when it came to a show-down. You were one of them, Fingers. I heard the story one Winter far north. I've kept it to myself, because I've sort of had the idea that you didn't want people to know or you would have told it yourself. That's why I wanted you to come to see me, Fingers. You know the situation. It's either the noose or iron bars for me. Naturally one would seek for assistance among those who have been his friends. But I do not, with the exception of Father Layonne. Just friendship won't save me, not the sort of friendship we have today. That's why I sent for you. Don't think that I am prying into secrets that are sacred to you, Fingers. God knows I don't mean it that way. But I've got to tell you of a thing that happened a long time ago, before you can understand. You haven't forgotten—you will never forget—Ben Tatman?"

As Kent spoke the name, a name which Dirty Fingers had heard no lips but his own speak aloud in nearly a quarter of a century, a strange and potent force seemed suddenly to take possession of the forest bencher's huge and flabby body. It rippled over and through him like an electrical voltaism, making his body rigid, stiffening what had seemed to be fat into muscle, tensing his hands until they knotted themselves slowly into fists. The wheeze went out of his breath, and it was the voice of another man who answered Kent.

"You have heard—about—Ben Tatman?"

"Yes. I heard it away up in the Porcupine country. They say it happened twenty years ago or more. This Tatman, so I was told, was a young fellow green from San Francisco—a bank clerk, I think—who came into the gold country and brought his wife with him. They were both chuck-full of courage, and the story was that each worshiped the ground the other walked on, and that the girl had insisted on being her husband's comrade in adventure. Of course neither guessed the sort of thing that was ahead of them.

"Then came that death Winter in Lost City. You know better than I what the laws were in those days, Fingers. Food failed to come up. Snow came early, the thermometer never rose over fifty below zero for three straight months, and Lost City was an inferno of starvation and death. You could go out and kill a man, then, and perhaps get away with it, Fingers. But if you stole so much as a crust of bread or a single bean, you were taken to the edge of the camp and told to go! And that meant certain death—death from hunger and cold, more terrible than shooting or hanging, and for that reason it was the penalty for theft.

"Tatman wasn't a thief. It was seeing his young wife slowly dying of hunger, and his horror at the thought of seeing her fall, as others were falling, a victim to scurvy, that made him steal. He broke into a cabin in the dead of night and stole two cans of beans and a pan of potatoes, more precious than a thousand times their weight in gold. And he was caught. Of course, there was the wife. But those were the days when a woman couldn't save a man, no matter how lovely she was. Tatman was taken to the edge of camp and given his pack and his gun—but no food. And the girl, hooded and booted, was at his side, for she was determined to die with him. For her sake Tatman had lied up to the last minute, protesting his innocence.

"But the beans and the potatoes were found in his cabin, and that was evidence enough. And then, just as they were about to go straight out into the blizzard that meant death within a few hours, then—"

Kent rose to his feet, and walked to the little window, and stood there, looking out. "Fingers, now and then a superman is born on earth. And a superman was there in that crowd of hunger-stricken and embittered men. At the last moment he stepped out and in a loud voice declared that Tatman was innocent and that he was guilty. Unafraid, he made a remarkable confession. He had stolen the beans and the potatoes and had slipped them into the Tatman cabin when they were asleep. Why? Because he wanted to save the woman from hunger! Yes, he lied, Fingers. He lied because he loved the wife that belonged to another man—lied because in him there was a heart as true as any heart God ever made. He lied! And his lie was a splendid thing. He went out into that blizzard, strengthened by a love that was greater than his fear of death, and the camp never heard of him again. Tatman and his wife returned to their cabin and lived. Fingers—" Kent whirled suddenly from the window. "Fingers—"

And Fingers, like a sphynx, sat and stared at Kent.

"You were that man," Kent went on, coming nearer to him. "You lied, because you loved a woman, and you went out to face death because of that woman. The men at Lost City didn't know it, Fingers. The husband didn't know it. And the girl, that girl-wife you worshiped in secret, didn't dream of it! But that was the truth, and you know it deep down in your soul. You fought your way out. You lived! And all these years, down here on your porch, you've been dreaming of a woman, of the girl you were willing to die for a long time ago. Fingers, am I right? And if I am, will you shake hands?"

Slowly Fingers had risen from his chair. No longer were his eyes dull and lifeless, but flaming with a fire that Kent had lighted again after many years. And he reached out a hand and gripped Kent's, still staring at him as though something had come back to him from the dead.

"I thank you, Kent, for your opinion of that man," he said. "Somehow, you haven't made me—ashamed. But it was only the shell of a man that won out after that day when I took Tatman's place. Something happened. I don't know what. But—you see me now. I never went back into the diggings. I degenerated. I became what I am."

"And you are today just what you were when you went out to die for Mary Tatman," cried Kent. "The same heart and the same soul are in you. Wouldn't you fight again today for her?"

A stifled cry came from Fingers' lips. "My God, yes, Kent—I would!"

"And that's why I wanted you, of all men, to come to me, Fingers," Kent went on swiftly. "To you, of all the men on earth, I wanted to tell my story. And now, will you listen to it? Will you forgive me for bringing up this memory that must be precious to you, only that you might more fully understand what I am going to say? I don't want you to think of it as a subterfuge on my part. It is more than that. It is—Fingers, is it inspiration? Listen, and tell me."

And for a long time after that James Kent talked, and Fingers listened, the soul within him writhing and dragging itself back into fierce life, demanding for the first time in many years the something which it had once possessed, but which it had lost. It was not the lazy, mysterious, silent Dirty Fingers who sat in the cell with Kent. In him the spirit of twenty years ago had roused itself from long slumber, and the thrill of it pounded in his blood. Two-Fisted Fingers they had called him then, and he was Two-Fisted Fingers in this hour with Kent. Twice Father Layonne came to the head of the cell alcove, but turned back when he heard the low and steady murmur of Kent's voice. Nothing did Kent keep hidden, and when he had finished, something that was like the fire of a revelation had come into Fingers' face.

"My God!" he breathed deeply. "Kent, I've been sitting down there on my porch a long time, and a good many strange things have come to me, but never anything like this. Oh, if it wasn't for this accursed flesh of mine!"

He jumped from his chair more quickly than he had moved in ten years, and he laughed as he had not laughed in all that time. He thrust out a great arm and doubled it up, like a prizefighter testing his muscle. "Old? I'm not old! I was only twenty-eight when that happened up there, and I'm forty-eight now. That isn't old. It's what is in me that's grown old. I'll do it, Kent! I'll do it, if I hang for it!"

Kent fairly leaped upon him. "God bless you!" he cried huskily. "God bless you, Fingers! Look! Look at that!" He pulled Fingers to the little window, and together they looked out upon the river, shimmering gloriously under a sun-filled sky of blue. "Two thousand miles of it," he breathed. "Two thousand miles of it, running straight through the heart of that world we both have known! No, you're not old, Fingers. The things you used to know are calling you again, as they are calling me, for somewhere off there are the ghosts of Lost City, ghosts—and realities!"

"Ghosts—and hopes," said Fingers.

"Hopes make life," softly whispered Kent, as if to himself. And then, without turning from the window, his hand found Fingers' and clasped it tight. "It may be that mine, like yours, will never come true. But they're fine to think about, Fingers. Funny, isn't it, that their names should be so strangely alike— Mary and Marette? I say, Fingers—"

Heavy footsteps sounded in the hall. Both turned from the window as Constable Pelly came to the door of the cell. They recognized this intimation that their time was up, and with his foot Fingers roused his sleeping dog.

It was a new Fingers who walked back to the river five minutes later, and it was an amazed and discomfited dog who followed at his heels, for at times the misshapen and flesh-ridden Togs was compelled to trot for a few steps to keep up. And Fingers did not sink into the chair on the shady porch when he reached his shack. He threw off his coat and waistcoat and rolled up his sleeves, and for hours after that he was buried deep in the accumulated masses of dust-covered legal treasures stored away in hidden corners of the Good Old Queen Bess.

CHAPTER XII

That morning Kent had heard wild songs floating up from the river, and now he felt like shouting forth his own joy and exultation in song. He wondered if he could hide the truth from the eyes of others, and especially from Kedsty if he came to see him. It seemed that some glimmer of the hope blazing within him must surely reveal itself, no matter how he tried to hold it back. He felt the vital forces of that hope more powerful within him now than in the hour when he had crept from the hospital window with freedom in his face. For then he was not sure of himself. He had not tested his physical strength. And in the present moment, fanned by his unbounded optimism, the thought came to him that perhaps it was good luck and not bad that had thrown Mercer in his way. For with Fingers behind him now, his chances for a clean get-away were better. He would not be taking a hazardous leap chanced on the immediate smiles of fortune. He would be going deliberately, prepared.

He blessed the man who had been known as Dirty Fingers, but whom he could not think of now in the terms of that name. He blessed the day he had heard that chance story of Fingers, far north. He no longer regarded him as the fat pig of a man he had been for so many years. For he looked upon the miracle of a great awakening. He had seen the soul of Fingers lift itself up out of its tabernacle of flesh and grow young again; he had seen stagnant blood race with new fire. He had seen emotions roused that had slept for long years. And he felt toward Fingers, in the face of that awakening, differently than he had felt toward any other living man. His emotion was one of deep and embracing comradeship.

Father Layonne did not come again until afternoon, and then he brought information that thrilled Kent. The missioner had walked down to see Fingers, and Fingers was not on his porch. Neither was the dog. He had knocked loudly on the door, but there was no answer. Where was Fingers? Kent shook his head, feigning an anxious questioning, but inside him his heart was leaping. He knew! He told Father Layonne he was afraid all Fingers' knowledge of the law could do him but little good, that Fingers had told him as much, and the little missioner went away considerably depressed. He would talk with Fingers again, he said, and offer certain suggestions he had in mind. Kent chuckled when he was gone. How shocked *le Pere* would be if he, too, could know!

The next morning Father Layonne came again, and his information was even more thrilling to Kent. The missioner was displeased with Fingers. Last night, noticing a light in his shack, he had walked down to see him. And he had found three men closely drawn up about a table with Dirty Fingers. One of them was Ponte, the half-breed; another was Kinoo the outcast Dog Rib from over on Sand Creek; the third was Mooie, the old Indian trailer. Kent wanted to jump up and shout, for those three were the three greatest trailers in all that part of the Northland. Fingers had lost no time, and he wanted to voice his approbation like a small boy on the Fourth of July.

But his face, seen by Father Layonne, betrayed none of the excitement that was in his blood. Fingers had told him he was going into a timber deal with these men, a long-distance deal where there would be much traveling, and that he could not interrupt himself just then to talk about Kent. Would Father Layonne come again in the morning? And he had gone again that morning, and Fingers' place was locked up!

All the rest of the day Kent waited eagerly for Fingers. For the first time Kedsty came to see him, and as a matter of courtesy said he hoped Fingers might be of assistance to him. He did not mention Mercer and remained no longer than a couple of minutes, standing outside the cell. In the afternoon Doctor Cardigan came and shook hands warmly with Kent. He had found a tough job waiting for him, he said. Mercer was all cut up, in a literal as well as a mental way. He had five teeth missing, and he had to have seventeen stitches taken in his face. It was Cardigan's opinion that some one had given him a considerable beating—and he grinned at Kent. Then he added in a whisper,

"My God, Kent, how I wish you had made it!"

It was four o'clock when Fingers came. Even less than yesterday did he look like the old Fingers. He was not wheezing. He seemed to have lost flesh. His face was alive. That was what struck Kent—the new life in it. There was color in his eyes. And Togs, the dog, was not with him. He smiled when he shook hands with Kent, and nodded, and chuckled. And Kent, after that, gripped him by the shoulders and shook him in his silent joy.

"I was up all last night," said Fingers in a low voice. "I don't dare move much in the day, or people will wonder. But, God bless my soul!—I did move last night, Kent. I must have walked ten miles, more or less. And things are coming—coming!"

"And Ponte, Kinoo, Mooie—?"

"Are working like devils," whispered Fingers. "It's the only way, Kent. I've gone through all my law, and there's nothing in man-made law that can save you. I've read your confession, and I don't think you could even get off with the penitentiary. A noose is already tied around your neck. I think you'd hang. We've simply got to get you out some other way. I've had a talk with Kedsty. He has made arrangements to have you sent to Edmonton two weeks from tomorrow. We'll need all that time, but it's enough."

For three days thereafter Fingers came to Kent's cell each afternoon, and each time was looking better. Something was swiftly putting hardness into his flesh and form into his body. The second day he told Kent that he had found the way at last, and that when the hour came, escape would be easy, but he thought it best not to let Kent in on the little secret just yet. He must be patient and have faith. That was the chief thing, to have faith at all times, no matter what happened. Several times he emphasized that "no matter what happens." The third day he puzzled Kent. He was restless, a bit nervous. He still thought it best not to tell Kent what his scheme was, until to-morrow. He was in the cell not more than five or ten minutes, and there was an unusual pressure in the grip of his hand when he bade Kent good-by. Somehow Kent did not feel so well when he had gone. He waited impatiently for the next day. It came, and hour after hour he listened for Fingers' heavy tread in the hall. The morning passed. The afternoon lengthened. Night came, and Fingers had not come. Kent did not sleep much between the hour when he went to bed and morning. It was eleven o'clock when the missioner made his call. Before he left, Kent gave him a brief note for Fingers. He had just finished his dinner, and Carter had taken the dishes away, when Father Layonne returned. A look at his face, and Kent knew that he bore unpleasant tidings.

"Fingers is an—an apostate," he said, his lips twitching as if to keep back a denunciation still more emphatic. "He was sitting on his porch again this morning, half asleep, and says that after a great deal of thought he has come to the definite opinion that he can do nothing for you. He read your note and burned it with a match. He asked me to tell you that the scheme he had in mind was too risky—for him. He says he won't come up again. And—"

The missioner was rubbing his brown, knotted hands together raspingly.

"Go on," said Kent a little thickly.

"He has also sent Inspector Kedsty the same word," finished Father Layonne. "His word to Kedsty is that he can see no fighting chance for you, and that it is useless effort on his part to put up a defense for you. Jimmy!" His hand touched Kent's arm gently.

Kent's face was white. He faced the window, and for a space he did not see. Then with pencil and paper he wrote again to Fingers.

It was late in the afternoon before Father Layonne returned with an answer. Again it was verbal. Fingers had read his note and had burned it with a match. He was particular that the last scrap of it was turned into ash, the missioner said. And he had nothing to say to Kent that he had not previously said. He simply could not go on with their plans. And he requested Kent not to write to him again. He was sorry, but that was his definite stand in the matter.

Even then Kent could not bring himself to believe. All the rest of the day he tried to put himself in Fingers' brain, but his old trick of losing his personality in that of another failed him this time. He could find no reason for the sudden change in Fingers, unless it was what Fingers had frankly confessed to Father Layonne—fear. The influence of mind, in this instance, had failed in its assault upon a mass of matter. Fingers' nerve had gone back on him.

The fifth day Kent rose from his cot with hope still not quite dead in his heart. But that day passed and the sixth, and the missioner brought word that Fingers was the old Dirty Fingers again, sitting from morning till night on his porch.

On the seventh day came the final crash to Kent's hopes. Kedsty's program had changed. He, Kent, was to start for Edmonton the following morning under charge of Pelly and a special constable!

After this Kent felt a strange change come over him. Years seemed to multiply themselves in his body. His mind, beaten back, no longer continued in its old channels of thought. The thing pressed upon him now as fatalistic. Fingers had failed him. Fortune had failed him. Everything had failed, and for the first time in the weeks of his struggle against death and a thing worse than death, he cursed himself. There was a limit to optimism and a limit to hope. His limit was reached.

In the afternoon of this seventh day came a depressing gloom. It was filled with a drizzling rain. Hour after hour this drizzle kept up, thickening as the night came. He ate his supper by the light of a cell lamp. By eight o'clock it was black outside. In that blackness there was an occasional flash of lightning and rumble of thunder. On the roof of the barracks the rain beat steadily and monotonously.

His watch was in his hand—it was a quarter after nine o'clock, when he heard the door at the far exit of the hall open and close. He had heard it a dozen times since supper and paid no attention to it, but this time it was followed by a voice at the detachment office that hit him like an electrical shock. Then, a moment later, came low laughter. It was a woman who laughed.

He stood up. He heard the detachment office door close, and silence followed. The watch in his hand seemed ticking off the seconds with frantic noise. He shoved it into his pocket and stood staring out into the prison alcove. A few minutes later the office door opened again. This time it was not closed. He heard distinctly a few light, hesitating footsteps, and his heart seemed to stop its beating. They came to the head of the lighted alcove, and for perhaps the space of a dozen seconds there was silence again. Then they advanced.

Another moment, and Kent was staring through the bars into the glorious eyes of Marette Radisson!

CHAPTER XIII

In that moment Kent did not speak. He made no sound. He gave no sign of welcome, but stood in the middle of his cell, staring. If life had hung upon speech in those few seconds, he would have died, but everything he would have said, and more, was in his face. The girl must have seen it. With her two hands she was gripping at the bars of the cell and looking through at him. Kent saw that her face was pale in the lamp glow. In that pallor her violet eyes were like pools of black. The hood of her dripping raincoat was thrown partly back, and against the whiteness of her cheeks her hair glistened wet, and her long lashes were heavy with the rain.

Kent, without moving over the narrow space between them, reached out his hands and found his voice. "Marette!"

Her hands had tightened about the bars until they were bloodless. Her lips were parted. She was breathing quickly, but she did not smile; she made no response to his greeting, gave no sign even of recognition. What happened after that was so sudden and amazing that his heart stopped dead still. Without warning she stepped back from the cell and began to scream and then drew away from him, still facing him and still screaming, as if something had terrified her.

Kent heard the crash of a chair in the detachment office, excited voices, and the running of feet. Marette Radisson had withdrawn to the far corner of the alcove, and as Carter and Pelly ran toward her, she stood, a picture of horror, pointing at Kent's cell. The two constables rushed past her. Close behind them followed the special officer detailed to take Kent to Edmonton.

Kent had not moved. He was like one petrified. Close up against the bars came the faces of Pelly, Carter, and the special constable, filled with the expressions of men who had expected to look in upon tragedy. And then, behind their backs, Kent saw the other thing happen. Swift as a flash Marette Radisson's hand went in and out of her raincoat, and at the backs of the three men she was leveling a revolver! Not only did Kent see that swift change, but the still swifter change that came into her face. Her eyes shot to his just once, and they were filled with a laughing, exultant fire. With one mighty throb Kent's heart seemed to leap out through the bars of his prison, and at the look in his face and eyes Carter swung suddenly around.

"Please don't make any disturbance, gentlemen," said Marette Radisson. "The first man that makes a suspicious move, I shall kill!"

Her voice was calm and thrilling. It had a deadly ring in it. The revolver in her hand was held steadily. It was a slim-barreled, black thing. The very color of it was menacing. And behind it were the girl's eyes, pools of flame. The three men were facing them now, shocked to speechlessness. Automatically they seemed to obey her command to throw up their hands. Then she leveled her grim little gun straight at Pelly's heart.

"You have the key," she said. "Unlock the cell!" Felly fumbled and produced the key. She watched him closely. Then suddenly the special constable dropped his arms with a coarse laugh. "A pretty trick," he said, "but the bluff won't work!"

"Oh, but it will!" came the reply.

The little black gun was shifted to him, even as the constable's fingers touched his revolver holster. With half-smiling lips, Marette's eyes blazed at him.

"Please put up your hands," she commanded.

The constable hesitated; then his fingers gripped the butt of his gun. Kent, holding his breath, saw the almost imperceptible tensing of Marette's body and the wavering of Pelly's arms over his head. Another moment and he, too, would have called the bluff if it were that. But that moment did not come. From the slim, black barrel of the girl's revolver leaped forth a sudden spurt of smoke and flame, and the special constable lurched back against the cell bars, caught himself as he half fell, and then stood with his pistol arm hanging limp and useless at his side. He had not made a sound, but his face was twisted in pain.

"Open the cell door!"

A second time the deadly-looking little gun was pointed straight at Pelly's heart. The half-smile was gone from the girl's lips now. Her eyes blazed a deeper fire. She was breathing quickly, and she leaned a little toward Pelly, repeating her command. The words were partly drowned in a sudden crash of thunder. But Pelly understood. He saw her lips form the words, and half heard,

"Open the door, or I shall kill you!"

He no longer hesitated. The key grated in the lock, and Kent himself flung the door wide open and sprang out. He was quick to see and seize upon opportunity and swift to act. The astounding audacity of the girl's ruse, her clever acting in feigning horror to line the guards up at the cell door and the thrilling decisiveness with which she had used the little black gun in her hand set every drop of blood in his body afire. No sooner was he outside his cell than he was the old Jim Kent, fighting man. He whipped Carter's automatic out of its holster and, covering Pelly and the special constable, relieved them of their guns. Behind him he heard Marette's voice, calm and triumphant,

"Lock them in the cell, Mr. Kent!"

He did not look at her, but swung his gun on Pelly and the special constable, and they backed through the door into the cell. Carter had not moved. He was looking straight at the girl, and the little black gun was leveled at his breast. Pelly and the wounded man did not see, but on Carter's lips was a strange smile. His eyes met Kent's, and there was revealed for an instant a silent flash of comradeship and an unmistakable something else. Carter was glad! It made Kent want to reach out and grip his hand, but in place of that he backed him into the cell, turned the key in the lock, and with the key in his hand faced Marette Radisson. Her eyes were shining gloriously. He had never seen such splendid, fighting eyes, nor the birdlike swiftness with which she turned and ran down the hall, calling him to follow her.

He was only a step behind her in passing Kedsty's office. She reached the outer door and opened it. It was pitch-dark outside, and a deluge of rain beat into their faces. He observed that she did not replace the hood of her raincoat when she darted out. As he closed the door, her hand groped to his arm and from that found his hand. Her fingers clung to his tightly.

He did not ask questions as they faced the black chaos of rain. A rending streak of lightning revealed her for an instant, her bare head bowed to the wind. Then came a crash of thunder that shook the earth under their feet, and her fingers closed more tightly about his hand. And in that crash he heard her voice, half laughing, half broken, saying,

"I'm afraid—of thunder!"

In that storm his laugh rang out, a great, free, joyous laugh. He wanted to stop in that instant, sweep her up into his arms, and carry her. He wanted to shout like an insane man in his mad joy. And a moment before she had risked everything in facing three of the bravest men in the service and had shot one of them! He started to say something, but she increased her speed until she was almost running.

She was not leading Jim in the direction of the river, but toward the forest beyond Kedsty's bungalow. Not for an instant did she falter in that drenched and impenetrable darkness. There was something imperative in the clasp of her fingers, even though they tightened perceptibly when the thunder crashed. They gave Kent the conviction that there was no doubt in her mind as to the point she was striving for. He took advantage of the lightning, for each time it gave him a glimpse of her bare, wet head bowed to the storm, her white profile, and her slim figure fighting over the sticky earth under her feet.

It was this presence of her, and not the thought of escape, that exalted him now. She was at his side. Her hand lay close in his. The lightning gave him glimpses of her. He felt the touch of her shoulder, her arm, her body, as they drew close together. The life and warmth and thrill of her seemed to leap into his own veins through the hand he held. He had dreamed of her. And now suddenly she had become a part of him, and the glory of it rode overwhelmingly over all other emotions that were struggling in his brain— the glory of the thought that it was she who had come to him in the last moment, who had saved him, and who was now leading him to freedom through the crash of storm.

At the crest of a low knoll between barracks and Kedsty's bungalow she stopped for the first time. He had there, again, the almost irresistible impulse to reach out in the darkness and take her into his arms, crying out to her of his joy, of a happiness that had come to him greater even than the happiness of freedom. But he stood, holding her hand, his tongue speechless, and he was looking at her when the lightning revealed her again. In a rending flash it cut open the night so close that the hiss of it was like the passing of a giant rocket, and involuntarily she shrank against him, and her free hand caught his arm at the instant thunder crashed low over their heads. His own hand groped out, and in the blackness it touched for an instant her wet face and then her drenched hair.

"Marette," he cried, "where are we going?"

"Down there," came her voice.

Her hand had left his arm, and he sensed that she was pointing, though he could not see. Ahead of them was a chaotic pit of gloom, a sea of blackness, and in the heart of that sea he saw a light. He knew that it was a lamp in one of Kedsty's windows and that Marette was guiding herself by that light when she started down the slope with her hand still in his. That she had made no effort to withdraw it made him unconscious of the almost drowning discomfort of the fresh deluge of rain that beat their faces. One of her fingers had gripped itself convulsively about his thumb, like a child afraid of falling. And each time the thunder crashed that soft hold on his thumb tightened, and Kent's soul acclaimed.

They drew swiftly nearer to the light, for it was not far from the knoll to Kedsty's place. Kent's mind leaped ahead. A little west by north from the inspector's bungalow was Kim's Bayou and it was undoubtedly to the forest trail over which she had gone at least once before, on the night of the mysterious assault upon Mooie, that Marette was leading him. Questions began to rush upon him now, immediate demanding questions. They were going to the river. They must be going to the river. It was the quickest and surest way of escape. Had Marette prepared for that? And was she going with him?

He had no time to answer. Their feet struck the gravel path leading to the door of Kedsty's place, and straight up this path the girl turned, straight toward the light blazing in the window. Then, to his amazement, he heard in the sweep of storm her voice crying out in glad triumph,

"We're home!"

Home! His breath came in a sudden gulp. He was more than astounded. He was shocked. Was she mad or playing an amazingly improper joke? She had freed him from a cell to lead him to the home of the Inspector of Police, the deadliest enemy the world now held for him. He stopped, and Marette Radisson tugged at his hand, pulling him after her, insisting that he follow. She was clutching his thumb as though she thought he might attempt to escape.

"It is safe, M'sieu Jeems," she cried. "Don't be afraid!"

M'sieu Jeems! And the laughing note of mockery in her voice! He rallied himself and followed her up the three steps to the door. Her hand found the latch, the door opened, and swiftly they were inside. The lamp in the window was close to them, but for a space he could not see because of the water in his eyes. He blinked it out, drew a hand across his face, and looked at Marette. She stood three or four paces from him. Her face was very white, and she was panting as if hard-run for breath, but her eyes were shining, and she was smiling at him. The water was running from her in streams.

"You are wet," she said. "And I am afraid you will catch cold. Come with me!"

Again she was making fun of him just as she had made fun of him at Cardigan's! She turned, and he ran upstairs behind her. At the top she waited for him, and as he came up, she reached out her hand, as if apologizing for having taken it from him when they entered the bungalow. He held it again as she led him down the hall to a door farthest from the stair. This she opened, and they entered. It was dark inside, and the girl withdrew her hand again, and Kent heard her moving across the room. In that darkness a new and thrilling emotion possessed him. The air he was breathing was not the air he had breathed in the hall. In it was the sweet scent of flowers, and of something else—the faint and intangible perfume of a woman's room. He waited, staring. His eyes were wide when a match leaped into flame in Marette's fingers. Then he stood in the glow of a lamp.

He continued to stare in the stupidity of a shock to which he was not accustomed. Marette, as if to give him time to acquaint himself with his environment, was taking off her raincoat. Under it her slim little figure was dry, except where the water had run down from her uncovered head to her shoulders. He noticed that she wore a short skirt, and boots, adorably small boots of splendidly worked caribou. And then suddenly she came toward him with both hands reaching out to him.

"Please shake hands and say you're glad," she said. "Don't look so—so—frightened. This is my room and you are safe here."

He held her hands tight, staring into the wonderful, violet eyes that were looking at him with the frank and unembarrassed directness of a child's. "I—I don't understand," he struggled. "Marette, where is Kedsty?"

"He should be returning very soon."

"And he knows you are here, of course?"

She nodded. "I have been here for a month."

Kent's hands closed tighter about hers. "I—I don't understand," he repeated. "Tonight Kedsty will know that it was you who rescued me and you who shot Constable Willis. Good God, we must lose no time in getting away!"

"There is great reason why Kedsty dare not betray my presence in his house," she said quietly. "He would die first! And he will not suspect that I have brought you to my room, that an escaped murderer is hiding under the very roof of the Inspector of Police! They will search for you everywhere but here! Isn't it splendid? He planned it all, every move, even to the screaming in front of your cell—"

"You mean—Kedsty?"

She withdrew her hands and stepped back from him, and again he saw in her eyes a flash of the fire that had come into them when she leveled her gun at the three men in the prison alcove. "No, not Kedsty. He would hang you, and he would kill me, if he dared. I mean that great, big, funny-looking friend of yours, M'sieu Fingers!"

CHAPTER XIV

The manner in which Kent stared at Marette Radisson after her announcement that it was Dirty Fingers who had planned his escape must have been, he thought afterward, little less than imbecile. He had wronged Fingers, he believed. He had called him a coward and a backslider. In his mind he had reviled him for helping to raise his hopes to the highest pitch, only to smash them in the end. And all the time Dirty Fingers had been planning this! Kent began to grin. The thing was clear in a moment—that is, the immediate situation was clear—or he thought it was. But there were questions—one, ten, a hundred of them. They wanted to pile over the end of his tongue, questions that had little or nothing to do with Kedsty. He saw nothing now but Marette.

She had begun to take down her hair. It fell about her in wet, shining masses. Kent had never seen anything like it. It clung to her face, her neck, her shoulders and arms, and shrouded her slender body to her hips, lovely in its confusion. Little drops of water glistened in it like diamonds in the lamp glow, trickling down and dropping to the floor. It was like a glowing coat of velvety sable beaten by storm. Marette ran her arms up through it, shaking it out in clouds, and a mist of rain leaped out from it, some of it striking Kent in the face. He forgot Fingers. He forgot Kedsty. His brain flamed only with the electrifying nearness of her. It was the thought of her that had inspired the greatest hope in him. It was his dreams of her, somewhere on the Big River, that had given him his great courage to believe in the ultimate of things. And now time and space had taken a leap backward. She was not four or five hundred miles north. There was no long quest ahead of him. She was here, within a few feet of him, tossing the wet from that glorious hair he had yearned to touch, brushing it out now, with her back toward him, in front of her mirror.

And as he sat there, uttering no word, looking at her, the demands of the immense responsibility that had fallen upon him and of the great fight that lay ahead pounded within him with naked fists. Fingers had planned. She had executed. It was up to him to finish.

He saw her, not as a creature to win, but as a priceless possession. Her fight had now become his fight. The rain was beating against the window near him. Out there was blackness, the river, the big world. His blood leaped with the old fighting fire. They were going tonight; they must be going tonight! Why should they wait? Why should they waste time under Kedsty's roof when freedom lay out there for the taking? He watched the swift movements of her hand, listened to the silken rustle of the brush as it smoothed out her long hair. Bewilderment, reason, desire for action fought inside him.

Suddenly she faced him again. "It has just this moment occurred to me," she said, "that you haven't said 'Thank you.'"

So suddenly that he startled her he was at her side. He did not hesitate this time, as he had hesitated in his room at Cardigan's place. He caught her two hands in his, and with them he felt the soft, damp crush of her hair between his fingers. Words tumbled from his lips. He could not remember afterward all that he said. Her eyes widened, and they never for an instant left his own. Thank her! He told her what had happened to him—in the heart and soul of him—from the hour she had come to him at Cardigan's. He told her of dreams and plans, of his determination to find her again after he had escaped, if it took him all his life. He told her of Mercer, of his discovery of her visit to Kim's Bayou, of his scheme to follow her down the Three Rivers, to seek for her at Fort Simpson, to follow her to the Valley of Silent Men, wherever it was. Thank her! He held her hands so tight they hurt, and his voice trembled. Under the cloud of her hair a slow fire burned in Marette Radisson's cheeks. But it did not show in her eyes. They looked at him so steadily, so unfalteringly, that his own face burned before he had finished what was in his mind to say, and he freed her hands and stepped back from her again.

"Forgive me for saying all that," he entreated. "But it's true. You came to me there, at Cardigan's place, like something I'd always dreamed about, but never expected to find. And you came to me again, at the cell, like—"

"Yes, I know how I came," she interrupted him. "Through the mud and the rain, Mr. Kent. And it was so black I lost my way and was terrified to think that I might not find barracks. I was half an hour behind Mr. Fingers' schedule. For that reason I think Inspector Kedsty may return at any moment, and you must not talk so loud—or so much."

"Lord!" he breathed in a whisper. "I have said a lot in a short time, haven't I? But it isn't a hundredth part of what I want to get out of my system. I won't ask the million questions that want to be asked. But I must know why we are here. Why have we come to Kedsty's? Why didn't we make for the river? There couldn't be a better night to get away."

"But it is not so good as the fifth night from now will be," she said, resuming the task of drying her hair. "On that night you may go to the river. Our plans were a little upset, you know, by Inspector Kedsty's change in the date on which you were to leave for Edmonton. Arrangements have been made so that on the fifth night you may leave safely."

"And you?"

"I shall remain here." And then she added in a low voice that struck his heart cold, "I shall remain to pay Kedsty the price which he will ask for what has happened tonight."

"Good God!" he cried. "Marette!"

She turned on him swiftly. "No, no, I don't mean that he will hurt me," she cried, a fierce little note in her voice. "I would kill him before that! I'm sorry I told you. But you must not question me. You shall not!"

She was trembling. He had never seen her excited like that before, and as she stood there before him, he knew that he was not afraid for her in the way that had flashed into his mind. She had not spoken empty words. She would fight. She would kill, if it was necessary to kill. And he saw her, all at once, as he had not seen her before. He remembered a painting which he had seen a long time ago in Montreal. It was *L'Esprit de la Solitude*—The Spirit of the Wild—painted by Conné, the picturesque French-Canadian friend of Lord Strathcona and Mount Royal, and a genius of the far backwoods who had drawn his inspiration from the heart of the wilderness itself. And that painting stood before him now in flesh and blood, its crudeness gone, but the marvelous spirit it had breathed remaining. Shrouded in her tumbled hair, her lips a little parted, every line of her slender body vibrant with an emotion which seemed consuming her, her beautiful eyes aglow with its fire, he saw in her, as Conné must have seen at another time, the soul of the great North itself. She seemed to him to breathe of the God's country far down the Three Rivers; of its almost savage fearlessness; its beauty, its sunshine, and its storm; its tragedy, its pathos, and its song. In her was the courage and the glory of that North. He had seen; and now he felt these things, and the thrill of them swept over him like an inundation.

He had heard her soft laugh, she had made fun of him when he thought he was dying; she had kissed him, she had fought for him, she had clung in terror to his hand when the lightning flashed; and now she stood with her little hands clenched in her hair, like a storm about to break. A moment ago she was so near that he had almost taken her in his arms. Now, in an instant, she had placed something so vast between them that he would not have dared to touch her hand or her hair. Like sun and cloud and wind she changed, and for him each change added to the wonder of her. And now it was storm. He saw it in her eyes, her hands, her body. He felt the electrical nearness of it in those low-spoken, trembling words, "*You shall not!*" The room seemed surcharged for a moment with impending shock. And then his physical eyes took in again the slimness of her, seized upon the alluring smallness of her and the fact that he could have tossed her to the ceiling without great effort. And yet he saw her as one sees a goddess.

"No, I won't ask you questions, when you look at me like that," he said, finding his tongue. "I won't ask you what this price is that Kedsty may demand, because you're not going to pay it. If you won't go with me, I won't go. I'd rather stay here and be hung. I'm not asking you questions, so please don't shoot, but if you told me the truth, and you belong in the North, you're going back with me—or I'm not going. I'll not budge an inch."

She drew a deep breath, as if something had greatly relieved her. Again her violet eyes came out from the shadow into sunlight, and her trembling mouth suddenly broke into a smile. It was not apologetic. There was about it a quick and spontaneous gladness which she made no effort at all to conceal.

"That is nice of you," she said. "I'm glad to hear you say it. I never knew how pleasant it was to have some one who was willing to be hung for me. But you will go. And I will not go. There isn't time to explain all about it just now, for Inspector Kedsty will be here very soon, and I must dry my hair and show you your hiding-place—if you have to hide."

She began to brush her hair again. In the mirror Kent caught a glimpse of the smile still trembling on her lips.

"I'm not questioning you," he guarded himself again, "but if you could only understand how anxious I am to know where Kedsty is, how Fingers found you, why you made us believe you were leaving the Landing and then returned—and—how badly I want to know something about you—I almost believe you'd talk a little while you are drying your hair."

"It was Mooie, the old Indian," she said. "It was he who found out in some way that I was here, and then M'sieu Fingers came himself one night when the Inspector was away—got in through a window and simply said that you had sent him, when I was just about to shoot him. You see, I knew you weren't going to die. Kedsty had told me that. I was going to help you in another way, if M'sieu Fingers hadn't come. Inspector Kedsty was over there tonight, at his cabin, when the thing happened down there. It was a part of Fingers' scheme—to keep him out of the way."

Suddenly she grew rigid. The brush remained poised in her hair. Kent, too, heard the sound that she had heard. It was a loud tapping at one of the curtained windows, the tapping of some metallic object. And that window was fifteen feet above the ground!

With a little cry the girl threw down her brush, ran to the window, and raised and lowered the curtain once. Then she turned to Kent, swiftly dividing her hair into thick strands and weaving them into a braid.

"It is Mooie," she cried. "Kedsty is coming!"

She caught his hand and hurried him toward the head of the bed, where two long curtains were strung on a wire. She drew these apart. Behind them were what seemed to Kent an innumerable number of feminine garments.

"You must hide in them, if you have to," she said, the excited little tremble in her voice again. "I don't think it will come to that, but if it does, you must! Bury yourself way back in them, and keep quiet. If Kedsty finds you are here—"

She looked into his eyes, and it seemed to Kent that there was something which was very near to fear in them now.

"If he should find you here, it would mean something terrible for me," she went on, her hands creeping to his arms. "I can not tell you what it is now, but it would be worse than death. Will you promise to stay here, no matter what happens down there, no matter what you may hear? Will you—Mr. Kent?"

"Not if you call me Mr. Kent," he said, something thickening in his throat.

"Will you—Jeems? Will you—no matter what happens—if I promise—when I come back—to kiss you?"

Her hands slipped almost caressingly from his arms, and then she had turned swiftly and was gone through the partly open door, closing it after her, before he could give his promise.

CHAPTER XV

For a space he stood where she had left him, staring at the door through which she had gone. The nearness of her in those last few seconds of her presence, the caressing touch of her hands, what he had seen in her eyes, her promise to kiss him if he did not reveal himself—these things, and the thought of the splendid courage that must be inspiring her to face Kedsty now, made him blind even to the door and the wall at which he was apparently looking. He saw only her face, as he had seen it in that last moment—her eyes, the tremble of her lips, and the fear which she had not quite hidden from him. She was afraid of Kedsty. He was sure of it. For she had not smiled; there was no flicker of humor in her eyes, when she called him Jeems, an intimate use of the names Jim and James in the far North. It was not facetiously that she had promised to kiss him. An almost tragic seriousness had possessed her. And it was that seriousness that thrilled him—that, and the amazing frankness with which she had coupled the name Jeems with the promise of her lips. Once before she had called him Jeems. But it was M'sieu Jeems then, and there had been a bit of taunting laughter in her voice. Jim or James meant nothing, but Jeems—He had heard mothers call little children that, in moments of endearment. He knew that wives and sweethearts used it in that same way. For Jim and James were not uncommon names up and down the Three Rivers, even among the half-breeds and French, and Jeems was the closer and more intimate thing bred of it.

His heart was thumping riotously as he went to the door and listened. A little while ago, when she faced him with flashing eyes, commanding him not to question her, he had felt an abyss under his feet. Now he was on a mountain. And he knew that no matter what he heard, unless it was her cry for help, he would not go down.

After a little he opened the door a mere crack so that sound might come to him. She had not forbidden that. Through the crack he could see a dim glow of light in the lower hall. But he heard no sound, and it occurred to him that old Mooie could still run swiftly, and that it might be some time before Kedsty would arrive.

As he waited, he looked about the room. His first impression was that Marette must have lived in it for a long time. It was a woman's room, without the newness of sudden and unpremeditated occupancy. He knew that formerly it had been Kedsty's room, but nothing of Kedsty remained in it now. And then, as his wondering eyes beheld the miracle, a number of things struck him with amazing significance. He no longer doubted that Marette Radisson was of the far Northland. His faith in that was absolute. If there had been a last question in his mind, it was wiped away because she called him Jeems. Yet this room seemed to give the lie to his faith. Fascinated by his discovery of things, he drew away from the door and stood over the dressing-table in front of the mirror.

Marette had not prepared the room for him, and her possessions were there. It did not strike him as sacrilege to look at them, the many intimate little things that are mysteriously used in the process of a lady's toilette. It was their number and variety that astounded him. He might have expected them in the boudoir of the Governor General's daughter at Ottawa, but not here— and much less farther north. What he saw was of exquisite material and workmanship. And then, as if attracted by a magnet, his eyes were drawn to something else. It was a row of shoes neatly and carefully arranged on the floor at one side of the dressing-table.

He stared at them, astounded. Never had he seen such an array of feminine footwear intended for the same pair of feet. And it was not Northern footwear. Every individual little beauty in that amazing row stood on a high heel! Their variety was something to which he had long been a stranger. There were buttoned boots, laced boots, brown boots, black boots, and white boots, with dangerously high and fragile looking heels; there were dainty little white kid slippers, slippers with bows, slippers with cut steel buckles, and slippers with dainty ribbon ties; there were high-heeled oxfords and high-heeled patent leather pumps! He gasped. He reached over, moved by an automatic sort of impulse, and took a satiny little pump in his hand.

The size of it gave him a decidedly pleasant mental shock, and, beginning to feel like one prying into a sleeper's secrets, he looked inside it. The size was there—number three. And it had come from Favre's in Montreal! One after another he looked inside half a dozen others. And all of them had come from Favre's in Montreal. The little shoes, more than all else that he had seen or that had happened, sent a question pounding through his brain. Who was Marette Radisson?

And that question was followed by other questions, until they tumbled over one another in his head. If she was from Montreal, why was she going north? If she belonged in the North, if she was a part of it, why was she taking all of this apparently worthless footwear with her? Why had she come to Athabasca Landing? What was she to Kedsty? Why was she hiding under his roof? Why—

He stopped himself, trying to find some one answer in all that chaos of questions. It was impossible for him to take his eyes from the shoes. A thought seized him. Ludicrously he dropped upon his knees in front of the row and with a face growing hotter each moment examined them all. But he wanted to know. And the discovery he made was that most of the footwear had been worn, some of it so slightly, however, that the impression of the foot was barely visible.

He rose to his feet and continued his inquiry. Of course she had expected him to look about. One couldn't help seeing, unless one were blind. He would have cut off a hand before opening one of the dressing-table drawers. But Marette herself had told him to hide behind the curtains if it became necessary, and it was an excusable caution for him to look behind those curtains now, to see what sort of hiding-place he had. He returned to the door first and listened. There was still no sound from below. Then he drew the curtains apart, as Marette had drawn them. Only he looked longer. He would tell her about it when she returned, if the act needed an apology.

His impression was a man's impression. What he saw was a billowing, filmy mass of soft stuff, and out of it there greeted him the faintest possible scent of lilac sachet powder. He closed the curtains with a deep breath of utter joy and of consternation. The two emotions were a jumble to him. The shoes, all that mass of soft stuff behind the curtains, were exquisitely feminine. The breath of perfume had come to him straight out of a woman's soul. There were seduction and witchery to it. He saw Marette, an enrapturing vision of loveliness, floating before his eyes in that sacred and mysterious vestment of which he had stolen a half-frightened glimpse. In white—the white, cobwebby thing of laces and embroidery that had hung straight before his eyes—in white—with her glorious black hair, her violet eyes, her—

And then it was that the incongruity of the thing, the almost sheer impossibility of it, clashed in upon his vision. Yet his faith was not shaken. Marette Radisson was of the North. He could not disbelieve that, even in the face of these amazing things that confronted him.

Suddenly he heard a sound that was like the explosion of a gun under his feet. It was the opening and closing of the hall door—but mostly the closing. The slam of it shook the house and rattled the glass in the windows. Kedsty had returned, and he was in a rage. Kent extinguished the light so that the room was in darkness. Then he went to the door. He could hear the quick, heavy tread of Kedsty's feet After that came the closing of a second door, followed by the rumble of Kedsty's voice. Kent was disappointed.

The Inspector of Police and Marette were in a room too far distant for him to distinguish what was said. But he knew that Kedsty had returned to barracks and had discovered what had happened there. After an interval his voice was a steady rumble. It rose higher. He heard the crash of a chair. Then the voice ceased, and after it came the tramping of Kedsty's feet. Not once did he catch the sound of Marette's voice, but he was sure that in the interval of silence she was talking. Then Kedsty's voice broke forth more furiously than before. Kent's fingers dug into the sill of the door. Each moment added to his conviction that Marette was in danger. It was not physical violence he feared. He did not believe Kedsty capable of perpetrating that upon a woman. It was fear that he would take her to barracks. The fact that Marette had told him there was a powerful reason why Kedsty would not do this failed to assure him. For she had also told him that Kedsty would kill her, if he dared. He held himself in readiness. At a cry from her, or the first move on Kedsty's part to take her from the bungalow, he would give battle in spite of Marette's warning.

He almost hoped one of these two things would happen. As he stood there, listening, waiting, the thought became almost a prayer. He had Pelly's revolver. Within twenty seconds he could have Kedsty looking down the barrel of it. The night was ideal for escape. Within half an hour they would be on the river. They could even load up with provisions from Kedsty's place. He opened the door a little more, scarcely making an effort to combat the impulse that dragged him out. Marette must be in danger, or she would not have confessed to him that she was in the house of a man who would like to see her dead. Why she was there did not interest him deeply now. It was the fact of the moment that was moving him swiftly toward action.

The door below opened again, and Kent's body grew rigid. He heard Kedsty charging through the lower hall like a mad bull. The outer door opened, slammed shut, and he was gone.

Kent drew back into the darkness of his room. It was some moments before he heard Marette coming slowly up the stairs. She seemed to be groping her way, though there was a dim illumination out there. Then she came through the door into the blackness of her room.

"Jeems," she whispered.

He went to her. Her hands reached out, and again they rested on his arms.

"You—you didn't come down the stair?"

"No."

"You—didn't hear?"

"I heard no words. Only Kedsty's voice."

It seemed to him that her voice, when she spoke again, trembled with an immeasurable relief. "You were good, Jeems. I am glad."

In that darkness he could not see. Yet something reached into him, thrilling him, quickening his pulse with a thing to which his eyes were blind. He bent down. He found her lips upturned, offering him the sweetness of the kiss which was to be his reward; and as he felt their warmth upon his own, he felt also the slightest pressure of her hands upon his arms.

"He is gone. We will light the lamp again," she said then.

CHAPTER XVI

Kent stood still while Marette moved in that gloom, found matches, and lighted the lamp. He had not spoken a word after the kiss. He had not taken advantage of it. The gentle pressure of her hands had restrained him from taking her in his arms. But the kiss itself fired him with a wild and glorious thrill that was like a vibrant music to which every atom of life in his body responded. If he claimed his reward at all, he had expected her kiss to be perhaps indifferent, at least neutral. But the lips she had given him there in the darkness of the room were warm, living, breathing lips. They had not been snatched away from him too quickly. Their sweetness, for an instant, had lingered.

Then, in the lamp glow, he was looking into Marette Radisson's face. He knew that his own was aflame. He had no desire to hide its confession, and he was eager to find what lay in her own eyes. And he was astonished, and then startled. The kiss had not disturbed Marette. It was as if it had never happened.

She was not embarrassed, and there was no hint of color in her face. It was her deathly whiteness that startled him, a pallor emphasized by the dark masses of her hair, and a strange glow in her eyes. It was not a glow brought there by the kiss. It was fear, fading slowly out of them as he looked, until at last it was gone, and her lips trembled with an apologetic smile.

"He was very angry," she said. "How easily some men lose their tempers, don't they—Jeems?"

The little break in her voice, her brave effort to control herself, and the whimsical bit of smile that accompanied her words made him want to do what the gentle pressure of her hands had kept him from doing a few moments before—pick her up in his arms. What she was trying to hide he saw plainly. She had been in danger, a danger greater than that which she had quietly and fearlessly faced at barracks. And she was still afraid of that menace. It was the last thing which she wanted him to know, and yet he knew it. A new force swept through him. It was the force which comes of mastery, of possessorship, of fighting grimly against odds. It rose in a mighty triumph. It told him this girl belonged to him, that she was his to fight for. And he was going to fight. Marette saw the change that came into his face. For a moment after she had spoken there was silence between them. Outside the storm beat in a fiercer blast. A roll of thunder crashed over the bungalow. The windows rattled in a sweep of wind and rain. Kent, looking at her, his muscles hardening, his face growing grimmer, nodded toward the window at which Mooie's signal had come.

"It is a splendid night—for us," he said. "And we must go."

She did not answer.

"In the eyes of the law I am a murderer," he went on. "You saved me. You shot a man. In those same eyes you are a criminal. It is folly to remain here. It is sheer suicide for both of us. If Kedsty—"

"If Kedsty does not do what I told him to do to-night, I shall kill him!" she said.

The quietness of her words, the steadiness of her eyes, held him speechless. Again it seemed to him, as it had seemed to him in his room at Cardigan's place, that it was a child who was looking at him and speaking to him. If she had shown fear a few moments before, that fear was not revealed in her face now. She was not excited. Her eyes were softly and quietly beautiful. She amazed him and discomfited him. Against that child-like sureness he felt himself helpless. Its potency was greater than his strength and greater than his determination. It placed between them instantly a vast gulf, a gulf that might be bridged by prayer and entreaty, but never by force. There was no hint of excitement in her threat against Kedsty, and yet in the very calmness of it he felt its deadliness.

A whimsical half-smile was trembling on her lips again, and a warmer glow came into her eyes. "Do you know," she said, "that according to an old and sacred code of the North you belong to me?"

"I have heard of that code," he replied. "A hundred years ago I should have been your slave. If it exists today, I am happy."

"Yes, you see the point, Jeems, don't you? You were about to die, probably. I think they would have hanged you. And I saved your life. Therefore your life belongs to me, for I insist that the code still lives. You are my property, and I am going to do with you as I please, until I turn you over to the Rivers. And you are not going tonight. You shall wait here for Laselle and his brigade."

"Laselle—Jean Laselle?"

She nodded. "Yes, that is why you must wait. We have made a splendid arrangement. When Laselle and his brigade start north, you go with them. And no one will ever know. You are safe here. No one will think of looking for you under the roof of the Inspector of Police."

"But you, Marette!" He caught himself, remembering her injunction not to question her. Marette shrugged her slim shoulders the slightest bit and nodded for him to look upon what she knew he had already seen, her room.

"It is not uncomfortable," she said. "I have been here for a number of weeks, and nothing has happened to me. I am quite safe. Inspector Kedsty has not looked inside that door since the day your big red-headed friend saw me down in the poplars. He has not put a foot on the stair. That is the dead-line. And—I know—you are wondering. You are asking yourself a great many questions—*a bon droit*, M'sieu Jeems. You are burning up with them. I can see it. And I—"

There was something suddenly pathetic about her, as she sank into the big-armed, upholstered chair which had been Kedsty's favorite reading chair. She was tired, and for a moment it seemed to Kent that she was almost ready to cry. Her ringers twisted nervously at the shining end of the braid in her lap, and more than ever he thought how slim and helpless, she was, yet how gloriously unafraid, how unconquerable with that something within her that burned like the fire of a dynamo. The flame of that force had gone down now, as though the fire itself was dying out; but when she raised her eyes to him, looking up at him from out of the big chair, he knew that back of the yearning, child-like glow that lay in them the heart of that fire was living and unquenchable. Again, for him, she had ceased to be a woman. It was the soul of a child that lay in her wide-open, wonderfully blue eyes. Twice before he had seen that miracle, and it held him now, as it had held him that first time when she had stood with her back at Cardigan's door. And as it had changed then, so it changed now, slowly, and she was a woman again, with that great gulf of unapproachableness between them. But the yearning was still there, revealing itself to him, and yet, like the sun, infinitely remote from him.

"I wish that I might answer those questions for you," she said, in a voice that was low and tired. "I should like to have you know, because I—I have great faith in you, Jeems. But I cannot. It is impossible. It is inconceivable. If I did—" She made a hopeless little gesture. "If I told you everything, you would not like me any more. And I want you to like me—until you go north with M'sieu Jean and his brigade."

"And when I do that," cried Kent, almost savagely, "I shall find this place you call the Valley of Silent Men, if it takes me all my life."

It was becoming a joy for him to see the sudden flashes of pleasure that leaped into her eyes. She attempted no concealment. Whatever her emotions were they revealed themselves unaffectedly and with a simple freedom from embarrassment that swept him with an almost reverential worship. And what he had just said pleased her. Unreservedly her glowing eyes and her partly smiling lips told him that, and she said: "I am glad you feel that way, Jeems. And I think you would find it—in time. Because—"

Her little trick of looking at him so steadily, as if there was something inside him which she was trying to see more clearly, made him feel more helplessly than ever her slave. It was as if, in those moments, she forgot that he was of flesh and blood, and was looking into his heart to see what was there before she gave voice to things.

And then she said, still twisting her braid between her slim fingers, "You would find it—perhaps—because you are one who would not give up easily. Shall I tell you why I came to see you at Doctor Cardigan's? It was curiosity, at first—largely that. Just why or how I was interested in the man you freed is one of the things I can not tell you. And I can not tell you why I came to the Landing. Nor can I say a word about Kedsty. It may be, some day, that you will know. And then you will not like me. For nearly four years before I saw you that day I had been in a desolation. It was a terrible place. It ate my heart and soul out with its ugliness, its loneliness, its emptiness. A little while longer and I would have died. Then the thing happened that brought me away. Can you guess where it was?"

He shook his head, "No."

"To all the others it was a beautiful place, Montreal."

"You were at school there?" he guessed.

"Yes, the Villa Maria. I wasn't quite sixteen then. They were kind. I think they liked me. But each night I prayed one prayer. You know what the Three Rivers are to us, to the people of the North. The Athabasca is Grandmother, the Slave is Mother, the Mackenzie is Daughter, and over them watches always the goddess Niska, the Gray Goose. And my prayer was that I might go back to them. In Montreal there were people, people everywhere, thousands and tens of thousands of them, so many that I was lonely and heartsick and wanted to get away. For the Gray Goose blood is in me, Jeems. I love the forests. And Niska's God doesn't live in Montreal. Her sun doesn't rise there. Her moon isn't the same there. The flowers are not hers. The winds tell different stories. The air is another air. People, when they look at you, look in another way. Away down the Three Rivers I had loved men. There I was learning to hate them. Then, something happened. I came to Athabasca Landing. I went to see you because—"

She clasped her two hands tightly in her lap. "Because, after those four terrible years, you were the first man I found who was playing a great, big, square game to the end. Don't ask me how I found it out. Please don't ask me anything. I am telling you all you can know, all you *shall* know. But I did find it out. And then I learned that you were not going to die. Kedsty told me that. And when I had talked with you I knew that you would play any game square, and I made up my mind to help you. That is why I am telling you all this—just to let you know that I have faith in you, and that you must not break that faith. You must not insist on knowing more about me. You must still play the game. I am playing mine, and you must play yours. And to play yours clean, you must go with Laselle's brigade and leave me with Kedsty. You must forget what has happened. You must forget what MAY happen. You can not help me. You can only harm me. And if—some day, a long time from now—you should happen to find the Valley of Silent Men—"

He waited, his heart pounding like a fist.

"I may—be there," she finished, in a voice so low that it was scarcely above a whisper.

It seemed to him that she was looking a long way off, and it was not in his direction. And then she smiled, not at him, but in a half-hopeless little way.

"I think I shall be disappointed if you don't find it," she said then, and her eyes were pure as the blue flowers from which they had stolen their color, as she looked at him. "You know the great Sulphur Country beyond Fort Simpson, westward between the Two Nahannis?"

"Yes. That is where Kilbane and his patrol were lost. The Indians call it the Devil Country. Is that it?"

She nodded. "They say no living thing has ever been through the Sulphur Country," she said. "But that is not true. I have been through it. It is beyond the Sulphur Country you must go to find the Valley of Silent Men, straight through that gap between the North and the South Nahanni. That is the way *you* must go if you should ever find it, Jeems, for otherwise you would have to come down from Dawson or up from Skagway, and the country is so great that you would never come upon it in a thousand years. The police will not find you there. You will always be safe. Perhaps I shall tell you more before the Brigade comes. But that is all tonight. I may never tell you anything more. And you must not question me."

Speechless he had stood, all the life of his soul burning like a fire in his eyes as he looked at her and listened to her, and now, quietly and unexcitedly, he said:

"Marette, I am going to play this game as you want me to play it, because I love you. It is only honest for me to tell you in words what you must already know. And I am going to fight for you as long as there is a drop of blood in my body. If I go with Jean Laselle's brigade, will you promise me—"

His voice trembled. He was repressing a mighty emotion. But not by the quiver of one of her long lashes did Marette Radisson give evidence that she had even heard his confession of love. She interrupted him before he had finished.

"I can promise you nothing, no matter what you do. Jeems, Jeems, you are not like those other men I learned to hate? You will not INSIST? If you do—if you are like them—yes, you may go away from here tonight and not wait for Jean Laselle. Listen! The storm will not break for hours. If you are going to demand a price for playing the game as I want you to play it, you may go. You have my permission."

She was very white. She rose from the big chair and stood before him. There was no anger in her voice or gesture, but her eyes glowed like luminous stars. There was something in them which he had not seen before, and suddenly a thought struck his heart cold as ice.

With a low cry he stretched out his hands, "My God, Marette, I am not a murderer! I did not kill John Barkley!"

She did not answer him.

"You don't believe me," he cried. "You believe that I killed Barkley, and that now—a murderer—I dare to tell you that I love you!"

She was trembling. It was like a little shiver running through her. For only a flash it seemed to him that he had caught a glimpse of something terrible, a thing she was hiding, a thing she was fighting as she stood there with her two little clenched hands. For in her face, in her eyes, in the beating throb of her white throat he saw, in that moment, the almost hidden agony of a hurt thing. And then it was gone, even as he entreated again, pleading for her faith.

"I did not kill John Barkley!"

"I am not thinking of that, Jeems," she said. "It is of something—"

They had forgotten the storm. It was howling and beating at the windows outside. But suddenly there came a sound that rose above the monotonous tumult of it, and Marette started as if it had sent an electric shock through her. Kent, too, turned toward the window.

It was the metallic tap, tap, tapping which once before had warned them of approaching danger. And this time it was insistent. It was as if a voice was crying out to them from beyond the window. It was more than premonition—it was the alarm of a near and impending menace. And in that moment Kent saw Marette Radisson's hands go swiftly to her throat and her eyes leap with sudden fire, and she gave a little cry as she listened to the sound.

CHAPTER XVII

In ten seconds, it seemed to Kent, Marette Radisson was again the splendid creature who had held the three men at bay over the end of her little black gun at barracks. The sound of Mooie's second warning came at first as a shock. Accompanying it there was a moment of fear, of fear driven almost to the point of actual terror. Following it came a reaction so swift that Kent was dazed. Within those ten seconds the girl's slender body seemed to grow taller; a new light flamed in her face; her eyes, turning swiftly to him, were filled with the same fire with which they had faced the three constables. She was unafraid. She was ready to fight.

In such moments as these it was the quiet and dispassionate composure of her voice that amazed him most. It was musical in its softness now. Yet in that softness was a hidden thing. It was like velvet covering steel. She had spoken of Niska, the Gray Goose, the goddess of the Three Rivers. And he thought that something of the spirit of a goddess must be in Marette Radisson to give her the courage with which she faced him, even as the metallic thing outside tapped its warning again at the window.

"Inspector Kedsty is coming back," she said. "I did not think he would do that—tonight."

"He has not had time to go to barracks," said Kent.

"No. Possibly he has forgotten something. Before he arrives, I want to show you the nest I have made for you, Jeems. Come quickly!"

It was her first intimation that he was not to remain in her room, a possibility that had already caused him some inward embarrassment. She seized a number of matches, turned down her light, and hurried into the hall. Kent followed her to the end of this hall, where she paused before a low half-door that apparently opened into some sort of a space close under the sloping roof of the bungalow.

"It is an old storeroom," she whispered. "I have made it quite comfortable, I think. I have covered the window, so you may light the lamp. But you must see that no light shows under this door. Lock it on the inside, and be very quiet. For whatever you find in there you must thank M'sieu Fingers."

She pulled the door slightly open and gave him the matches. The illumination in the lower hall made its way only dimly to where they stood. In the gloom he found himself close to the soft glow of her eyes. His fingers closed about her hand as he took the matches.

"Marette, you believe me?" he entreated. "You believe that I love you, that I didn't kill John Barkley, that I am going to fight for you as long as God gives me breath to fight?"

For a moment there was silence. Her hand withdrew gently from his.

"Yes, I think that I believe. Good-night, Jeems."

She went from him quickly. At her door she turned. "Go in now, please," she called back softly. "If you care as you say you do, *go in*."

She did not wait for his reply. Her own door closed behind her, and Kent, striking a match, stooped low and entered his hiding-place. In a moment he saw directly ahead of him a lamp on a box. He lighted this, and his first movement then was to close the door and turn the key that was in the lock. After that he looked about him. The storeroom was not more than ten feet square, and the roof was so close over his head that he could not stand upright. It was not the smallness of the place that struck him first, but the preparations which Marette had made for him. In a corner was a bed of blankets, and the rough floor of the place was carpeted with blankets, except for a two-or-three-foot space around the edge of it. Beyond the box was a table and a chair, and it was the burden of this table that made his pulse jump quickest. Marette had not forgotten that he might grow hungry. It was laid sumptuously, with a plate for one, but with food for half a dozen. There were a brace of roasted grouse, brown as nuts; a cold roast of moose meat or beef; a dish piled high with golden potato salad; olives, pickles, an open can of cherries, a loaf of bread, butter, cheese—and one of Kedsty's treasured thermos bottles, which undoubtedly held hot coffee or tea. And then he noticed what was on the chair—a belt and holster and a Colt automatic forty-five! Marette had not figured on securing a gun in the affair at barracks, and her foresight had not forgotten a weapon. She had placed it conspicuously where he could not fail to see it at once. And just beyond the chair, on the floor, was a shoulder-pack. It was of the regulation service sort, partly filled. Resting against the pack was a Winchester. He recognized the gun. He had seen it hanging in Dirty Fingers' shack.

For a matter of five minutes he scarcely moved from where he stood beside the table. Nothing but an unplastered roof was between him and the storm, and over his head the thunder crashed, and the rain beat in torrents. He saw where the window was, carefully covered with a blanket. Even through the blanket he caught faintly the illumination of lightning. This window overlooked the entrance to Kedsty's bungalow, and the idea came to him of turning out the light and opening it. In darkness he took down the blanket. But the window itself was not movable, and after assuring himself of this fact he flattened his face against it, peering out into the chaos of the night.

In that instant came a flare of lightning, and to Kent, looking down, was revealed a sight that tightened every muscle in his body. More vividly than if it had been day he saw a man standing below in the deluge. It was not Mooie. It was not Kedsty. It was no one that he had ever seen. Even more like a ghost than a man was that apparition of the lightning flare. A great, gaunt giant of a ghost, bare-headed, with long, dripping hair and a long, storm-twisted beard. The picture shot to his brain with the swiftness of the lightning itself. It was like the sudden throwing of a cinema picture on a screen. Then blackness shut it out. Kent stared harder. He waited.

Again came the lightning, and again he saw that tragic, ghost-like figure waiting in the storm. Three times he saw it. And he knew that the mysterious, bearded giant was an old man. The fourth time the lightning came, the figure was gone. And in that flare it was the bowed figure of Kedsty he saw hurrying up the gravel path to the door.

Quickly Kent covered the window, but he did not relight the lamp. Before Kedsty could have reached the foot of the stair, he had unlocked the door. Cautiously he opened it three or four inches and sat down with his back against the wall, listening. He heard Kedsty pass through into the big room where Marette had waited for him a short time before. After that there was silence except for the tumult of the storm.

For an hour Kent listened. In all that time he did not hear a sound from the lower hall or from Marette's room. He wondered if she was sleeping, and if Kedsty had gone to bed, waiting for morning before he set in action his bloodhounds of the law.

Kent had no intention of disturbing the comfortable looking bed of blankets. He was not only sleepless, but filled with a premonition of events about to happen. He felt impinging itself more and more upon him a sense of watchfulness. That Inspector Kedsty and Marette Radisson were under the same roof, and that there was some potent and mysterious reason which kept Kedsty from betraying the girl's presence, was the thought which troubled him most. He was not developing further the plans for his own escape.

He was thinking of Marette. What was her power over Kedsty? Why was it that Kedsty would like to see her dead? Why was she in his house? Again and again he asked himself the questions and found no answers to them. And yet, even in this purgatory of mystery that environed him, he felt himself happier than he had ever been in his life. For Marette was not four or five hundred miles down the river. She was in the same house with him. And he had told her that he loved her. He was glad that he had been given courage to let her know that. He relighted the lamp, and opened his watch and placed it on the table, where frequently he could look at the time. He wanted to smoke his pipe, but the odor of tobacco, he was sure, would reach Kedsty, unless the Inspector had actually retired into his bedroom for the night.

Half a dozen times he questioned himself as to the identity of the ghostly apparition he had seen in the lightning flare of the storm. Perhaps it was some one of Fingers' strange friends from out of the wilderness, Mooie's partner in watching the bungalow. The picture of that giant of a man with his great beard and long hair, as his eyes had caught him in a sea of electrical fire, was indelibly burned into his brain. It was a tragic picture.

Again he put out the light and bared the blanketed window, but he saw nothing but the sodden gleam of the earth when the lightning flashed. A second time he opened the door a few inches and sat down with his back to the wall, listening.

How long it was before drowsiness stole upon him he did not know, but it came, and for a few moments at a time, as his eyes closed, it robbed him of his caution. And then, for a space, he slept. A sound brought him suddenly into wide wakefulness. His first impression was that the sound had been a cry. For a moment or two, as his senses adjusted themselves, he was not sure. Then swiftly the thing grew upon him.

He rose to his feet and widened the crack of his door. A bar of light shot across the upper hall. It was from Marette's room. He had taken off his boots to deaden the sound of his feet, and he stepped outside his door. He was positive he heard a low cry, a choking, sobbing cry, only barely audible, and that it came from down the stair.

No longer hesitating, he moved quickly to Marette's room and looked in. His first glimpse was of the bed. It had not been used. The room was empty. Something cold and chilling gripped at his heart, and an impulse which he no longer made an effort to resist pulled him to the head of the stair. It was more than an impulse—it was a demand. Step by step he went down, his hand on the butt of his Colt.

He reached the lower hall, which was still lighted, and a step or two brought him to a view of the door that opened into the big living-room beyond. That door was partly open, and the room itself was filled with light. Soundlessly Kent approached. He looked in.

What he saw first brought him relief together with shock. At one end of the long desk table over which hung a great brass lamp stood Marette. She was in profile to him. He could not see her face. Her hair fell loose about her, glowing like a rich, sable cape in the light of the lamp. She was safe, alive, and yet the attitude of her as she looked down was the thing that gave him shock. He was compelled to move a few inches more before he could see what she was staring at. And then his heart stopped dead still.

Huddled down in his chair, with his head flung back so that the terrible ghastliness of his face fronted Kent, was Kedsty. And Kent, in an instant, knew. Only a dead man could look like that.

With a cry he entered the room. Marette did not start, but an answering cry came into her throat as she turned her eyes from Kedsty to him. To Kent it was like looking upon the dead in two ways. Marette Radisson, living and breathing, was whiter than Kedsty, who was white with the unbreathing pallor of the actually dead. She did not speak. She made no sound after that answering cry in her throat. She simply looked. And Kent spoke her name gently as he saw her great, wide eyes blazing dully their agony and despair. Then, like one stunned and fascinated, she stared down upon Kedsty again.

Every instinct of the man-hunter became alive in Kent's brain as he, too, turned toward the Inspector of Police. Kedsty's arms hung limp over the side of his chair. On the floor under his right hand was his Colt automatic. His head was strained so far over the back of the chair that it looked as though his neck had been broken. On his forehead, close up against his short-cropped, iron-gray hair, was a red stain.

Kent approached and bent over him. He had seen death too many times not to recognize it now, but seldom had he seen a face twisted and distorted as Kedsty's was. His eyes were open and bulging in a glassy stare. His jaws hung loose. His—

It was then Kent's blood froze in his veins. Kedsty had received a blow, but it was not the blow that had killed him. Afterward he had been choked to death. And the thing that had choked him was *a tress of woman's hair.*

In the seconds that followed that discovery Kent could not have moved if his own life had paid the penalty of inaction. For the story was told—there about Kedsty's throat and on his chest. The tress of hair was long and soft and shining and black. It was twisted twice around Kedsty's neck, and the loose end rippled down over his shoulder, *glowing like a bit of rich sable in the lamplight.* It was that thought of velvety sable that had come to him at the doorway, looking at Marette. It was the thought that came to him now. He touched it; he took it in his fingers; he unwound it from about Kedsty's neck, where it had made two deep rings in the flesh. From his fingers it rippled out full length. And he turned slowly and faced Marette Radisson.

Never had human eyes looked at him as she was looking at him now. She reached out a hand, her lips mute, and Kent gave her the tress of hair. And the next instant she turned, with a hand clasped at her own throat, and passed through the door.

After that he heard her going unsteadily up the stairs.

CHAPTER XVIII

Kent did not move. His senses for a space were stunned. He was almost physically insensible to all emotions but that one of shock and horror. He was staring at Kedsty's gray-white, twisted face when he heard Marette's door close. A cry came from his lips, but he did not hear it—was unconscious that he had made a sound. His body shook with a sudden tremor. He could not disbelieve, for the evidence was there. From behind, as he had sat in his chair Marette Radisson had struck the Inspector of Police with some blunt object. The blow had stunned him. And after that—

He drew a hand across his eyes, as if to clear his vision. What he had seen was impossible. The evidence was impossible. Assaulted, in deadly peril, defending either honor or love, Marette Radisson was of the blood to kill. But to creep up behind her victim—it was inconceivable! Yet there had been no struggle. Even the automatic on the floor gave no evidence of that. Kent picked it up. He looked at it closely, and again the unconscious cry of despair came in a half groan from his lips. For on the butt of the Colt was a stain of blood and a few gray hairs. Kedsty had been stunned by a blow from his own gun!

As Kent placed it on the table, his eyes caught suddenly a gleam of steel under the edge of a newspaper, and he drew out from their hiding-place the long-bladed clipping scissors which Kedsty had used in the preparation of his scrap-books and official reports. It was the last link in the deadly evidence—the automatic with its telltale stain, the scissors, the tress of hair, and Marette Radisson. He felt a sensation of sudden dizziness. Every nerve-center in his body had received its shock, and when the shock had passed it left him sweating.

Swiftly the reaction came. It was a lie, he told himself. The evidence was false. Marette could not have committed that crime, as the crime had visualized itself before his eyes. There was something which he had not seen, something which he could not see, something that was hiding itself from him. He became, in an instant, the old James Kent. The instinctive processes of the man-hunter leaped to their stations like trained soldiers. He saw Marette again, as she had looked at him when he entered the room. It was not murder he had caught in her wide-open eyes. It was not hatred. It was not madness. It was a quivering, bleeding soul crying out to him in an agony that no other human eyes had ever revealed to him before. And suddenly a great voice cried out in his brain, drowning all other things, telling him how contemptible a thing was love unless in that love was faith.

With his heart choking him, he turned again to Kedsty. The futility of the thing which he had told himself was faith gripped at him sickeningly, yet he fought for that faith, even as his eyes looked again upon the ghastly torture that was in Kedsty's face.

He was becoming calmer. He touched the dead man's cheek and found that it was no longer warm. The tragedy must have occurred an hour before. He examined more closely the abrasion on Kedsty's forehead. It was not a deep wound, and the blow that had made it must have stunned the Inspector of Police for only a short time. In that space the other thing had happened. In spite of his almost superhuman effort to keep the picture away from him, Kent saw it vividly—the swift turning to the table, the inspiration of the scissors, the clipping of the long tress of hair, the choking to death of Kedsty as he regained consciousness. Over and over again he whispered to himself the impossibility of it, the absurdity of it, the utter incongruity of it. Only a brain gone mad would have conceived that monstrous way of killing Kedsty. And Marette was not mad. She was sane.

Like the eyes of a hunting ferret his own eyes swept quickly about the room. At the four windows there were long curtain cords. On the walls, hung there as trophies, were a number of weapons. On one end of Kedsty's desk, used as a paperweight, was a stone tomahawk. Still nearer to the dead man's hands, unhidden by papers, was a boot-lace. Under his limp right hand was the automatic. With these possible instruments of death close at hand, ready to be snatched up without trouble or waste of time, why had the murderer used a tress of woman's hair?

The boot-lace drew Kent's eyes. It was impossible not to see it, forty-eight inches long and quarter-inch-wide buckskin. He began seeking for its mate, and found it on the floor where Marette Radisson had been standing. And again the unanswerable question pounded in Kent's brain—why had Kedsty's murderer used a tress of hair instead of a buckskin lace or one of the curtain cords hanging conspicuously at the windows?

He went to each of these windows and found them locked. Then, a last time, he bent over Kedsty. He knew that in the final moments of his life Kedsty had suffered a slow and torturing agony. His twisted face left the story. And the Inspector of Police was a powerful man. He had struggled, still partly dazed by the blow. But it had taken strength to overcome him even then, to hold his head back, to choke life out of him slowly with the noose of hair. And Kent, now that the significance of what he saw began to grow upon him more clearly, felt triumphing over all other things in his soul a slow and mighty joy. It was inconceivable that with the strength of her own hands and body Marette Radisson had killed Kedsty. A greater strength than hers had held him in the death-chair, and a greater strength than hers had choked life from the Inspector of Police!

He drew slowly out of the room, closing the door noiselessly behind him. He found that the front door was as Kedsty had left it, unlocked.

Close to that door he stood for a space, scarcely allowing himself to breathe. He listened, but no sound came down the dimly illumined stairway.

A new thing was pressing upon him now. It rode over the shock of tragedy, over the first-roused instincts of the man-hunter, overwhelming him with the realization of a horror such as had never confronted him before. It gripped him more fiercely than the mere killing of Kedsty. His thought was of Marette, of the fate which dawn and discovery would bring for her. His hands clenched and his jaws tightened. The world was against him, and tomorrow it would be against her. Only he, in the face of all that condemning evidence in the room beyond, would disbelieve her guilty of Kedsty's death. And he, Jim Kent, was already a murderer in the eyes of the law.

He felt within him the slow-growing inspiration of a new spirit, the gathering might of a new force. A few hours ago he was an outcast. He was condemned. Life, for him, had been robbed of its last hope. And in that hour of his grimmest despair Marette Radisson had come to him. Through storm that had rocked the earth under her feet and set ablaze the chaotic blackness of the sky over her head she had struggled—for him. She had counted no cost. She had measured no chances. She had simply come—*because she believed in him*. And now, upstairs, she was the victim of the terrible price that was the first cost of his freedom. For he believed, now that the thought came to him like a dagger stroke, that this was so. Her act in freeing him had brought about the final climax, and as a result of it, Kedsty was dead.

He went to the foot of the stair. Quietly, in his shoeless feet, he began to climb them. He wanted to cry out Marette's name even before he came to the top. He wanted to reach up to her with his arms outstretched. But he came silently to her door and looked in.

She lay in a crumpled, huddled heap on her bed. Her face was hidden, and all about her lay her smothering hair. For a moment he was frightened. He could not see that she was breathing. So still was she that she was like one dead.

His footsteps were unheard as he moved across the room. He knelt down beside her, reached out his arms, and gathered her into them.

"Marette!" he cried in a low voice.

He felt the sudden quiver, like a little shock, that ran through her. He crushed his face down, so that it lay in her hair, still damp from its wetting. He drew her closer, tightening his arms about her slender body, and a little cry came from her a cry that was a broken thing, a sob without tears.

"Marette!"

It was all he said. It was all he could say in that moment when his heart was beating like a drum against her breast. And then he felt the slow pressure of her hands against him, saw her white face, her wide, staring eyes within a few inches of his own, and she drew away from him, back against the wall, still huddled like a child on the bed, with her eyes fixed on him in a way that frightened him. There were no tears in them. She had not been crying. But her face was as white as he had seen it down in Kedsty's room. Some of the horror and shock had gone out of it. In it was another look as her eyes glowed upon Kent. It was a look of incredulity, of disbelief, a thing slowly fading away under the miracle of an amazing revelation. The truth thrust itself upon him.

Marette had not expected that he would come to her like this. She had believed that he would take flight into the night, escaping from her as he would have run from a plague. She put up her two hands, in the trick they had of groping at her white throat, and her lips formed a word which she did not speak.

Kent, to his own amazement, was smiling and still on his knees. He pulled himself to his feet, and stood up straight, looking down at her in that same strange, comforting, all-powerful way. The thrill of it was passing into her veins. A flush of color was driving the deathly pallor from her face. Her lips were parted, and she breathed quickly, a little excitedly.

"I thought—you would go!" she said.

"Not without you," he said. "I have come to take you with me."

He drew out his watch. It was two o'clock. He held it down so that she could look at the dial.

"If the storm keeps up, we have three hours before dawn," he said. "How soon can you be ready, Marette?"

He was fighting to make his voice quiet and unexcited. It was a terrific struggle. And Marette was not blind to it. She drew herself from the bed and stood up before him, her two hands still clasped at her throbbing throat.

"You believe—that I killed Kedsty," she said in a voice that was forced from her lips. "And you have come to help me—to pay me for what I tried to do for you? That is it—Jeems?"

"Pay you?" he cried. "I couldn't pay you in a million years! From that day you first came to Cardigan's place you gave me life. You came when the last spark of hope in me had died. I shall always believe that I would have died that night. But you saved me.

"From the moment I saw you I loved you, and I believe it was that love that kept me alive. And then you came to me again, down there, through this storm. Pay you! I can't. I never shall be able to. Because you thought I had killed a man made no difference You came just the same. And you came ready to kill, if necessary—for me. I'm not trying to tell myself *why*! But you did. You were ready to kill. And I am ready to kill—tonight—for you! I haven't got time to think about Kedsty. I'm thinking about you. If you killed him, I'm just telling myself there was a mighty good reason for it. But I don't believe it was you who killed him. You couldn't do it—with those hands!"

He reached out suddenly and seized them, slipping his grip to her wrists, so that her hands lay upward in his own, hands that were small, slim-fingered, soft-palmed, beautiful.

"They couldn't!" he cried, almost fiercely. "I swear to God they couldn't!"

Her eyes and face flamed at his words. "You believe that, Jeems?"

"Yes, just as you believe that I did not kill John Barkley. But the world is against us. It is against us both now. And we've got to hunt that hidden valley of yours together. Understand, Marette? And I'm—rather glad."

He turned toward the door. "Will you be ready in ten minutes?" he asked.

She nodded. "Yes, in ten minutes."

He ran out into the hall and down the stair, locking the front door. Then he returned to his hiding-place under the roof. He knew that a strange sort of madness was in his blood, for in the face of tonight's tragedy only madness could inspire him with the ecstatic thrill that was in his veins. Kedsty's death seemed far removed from a more important thing—the fact that from this hour Marette was his to fight for, that she belonged to him, that she must go with him. He loved her. In spite of whoever she was and whatever she had done, he loved her. Very soon she would tell him what had happened in the room below, and the thing would be clear.

There was one little corner of his brain that fought him. It kept telling him, like a parrot, that it was a tress of Marette's hair about Kedsty's throat, and that it was the hair that had choked him. But Marette would explain that, too. He was sure of it. In the face of the facts below he was illogical and unreasonable. He knew it. But his love for this girl, who had come strangely and tragically into his life, was like an intoxicant. And his faith was illimitable. She did not kill Kedsty. Another part of his brain kept repeating that over and over, even as he recalled that only a few hours before she had told him quite calmly that she would kill the Inspector of Police—if a certain thing should happen.

His hands worked as swiftly as his thoughts. He laced up his service boots. All the food and dishes on the table he made into a compact bundle and placed in the shoulder-pack. He carried this and the rifle out into the hall. Then he returned to Marette's room. The door was closed. At his knock the girl's voice told him that she was not quite ready.

He waited. He could hear her moving about quickly in her room. An interval of silence followed. Another five minutes passed—ten—fifteen. He tapped at the door again. This time it was opened.

He stared, amazed at the change in Marette. She had stepped back from the door to let him enter, and stood full in the lamp-glow. Her slim, beautiful body was dressed in a velvety blue corduroy; the coat was close-fitting and boyish; the skirt came only a little below her knees. On her feet were high-topped caribou boots. About her waist was a holster and the little black gun. Her hair was done up and crowded under a close-fitting turban. She was exquisitely lovely, as she stood there waiting for him, and in that loveliness Kent saw there was not one thing out of place. The corduroy, the turban, the short skirt, and the high, laced boots were made for the wilderness. She was not a tenderfoot. She was a little *sourdough*—clear through! Gladness leaped into Kent's face. But it was not the transformation of her dress alone that amazed him. She was changed in another way. Her cheeks were flushed. Her eyes glowed with a strange and wonderful radiance as she looked at him. Her lips were red, as he had seen them that first time at Cardigan's place. Her pallor, her fear, her horror were gone, and in their place was the repressed excitement of one about to enter upon a strange adventure.

On the floor was a pack only half as large as Kent's and when he picked it up, he found it of almost no weight. He fastened it to his own pack while Marette put on her raincoat and went down the stair ahead of him. In the hall below she was waiting, when he came down, with Kedsty's big rubber slicker in her hands.

"You must put it on," she said.

She shuddered slightly as she held the garment. The color was almost gone from her cheeks, as she faced the door beyond which the dead man sat in his chair, but the marvelous glow was still in her eyes as she helped Kent with his pack and the slicker and afterward stood for an instant with her hands touching his breast and her lips as if about to speak something which she held back.

A few steps beyond them they heard the storm. It seemed to rush upon the bungalow in a new fury, beating at the door, crashing over their heads in thunder, daring them to come out. Kent reached up and turned out the hall light.

In darkness he opened the door. Rain and wind swept in. With his free hand he groped out, found Marette, drew her after him, and closed the door again. Entering from the lighted hall into the storm was like being swallowed in a pit of blackness. It engulfed and smothered them. Then came suddenly a flash of lightning, and he saw Marette's face, white and drenched, but looking at him with that same strange glow in her eyes. It thrilled him. Even in the darkness it was there. It had been there since he had returned to her from Kedsty and had knelt at her bedside, with his arms about her for a moment.

Only now, in the beat of the storm, did an answer to the miracle of it come to him. It was because of *him*. It was because of his *faith* in her. Even death and horror could not keep it from her eyes. He wanted to cry out the joy of his discovery, to give wild voice to it in the teeth of the wind and the rain. He felt sweeping through him a force mightier than that of the night. Her hands were on his arm, as if she was afraid of losing him in that pit of blackness; the soft cling of them was like a contact through which came a warm thrill of electrical life. He put out his arm and drew her to him, so that for a moment his face pressed against the top of her wet little turban.

And then he heard her say: "There is a scow at the bayou, Jeems. It is close to the end of the path. M'sieu Fingers has kept it there, waiting, ready."

He had been thinking of Crossen's place and an open boat. He blessed Fingers again, as he took Marette's hand in his own and started for the trail that led through the poplar thicket.

Their feet slopped deep in wet and mud, and with the rain there was a wind that took their breath away. It was impossible to see a tree an arm's length away, and Kent hoped that the lightning would come frequently enough to guide him. In the first flare of it he looked down the slope that led riverward. Little rivulets of water were running down it. Rocks and stumps were in their way, and underfoot it was slippery. Marette's fingers were clinging to his again, as she had held to them on the wild race up to Kedsty's bungalow from the barracks. He had tingled then in the sheer joy of their thrill, but it was a different thrill that stirred him now—an overwhelming emotion of possessorship. This night, with its storm and its blackness, was the most wonderful of all his nights.

He sensed nothing of its discomfort. It could not beat back the joyous racing of the blood in his body. Sun and stars, day and night, sunshine and cloud, were trivial and inconsequential to him now. For close to him, struggling with him, fighting through the night with him, trusting him, helpless without him, was the living, breathing thing he loved more than he loved his own life. For many years, without knowing it, he had waited for this night, and now that it was upon him, it inundated and swept away his old life. He was no longer the huntsman, but the hunted. He was no longer alone, but had a priceless thing to fight for, a priceless and helpless thing that was clinging to his fingers in the darkness. He did not feel like a fugitive, but as one who has come into a great triumph. He sensed no uncertainty or doubt.

The river lay ahead, and for him the river had become the soul and the promise of life. It was Marette's river and his river, and in a little while they would be on it. And Marette would then tell him about Kedsty. He was sure of that. She would tell him what had happened while he slept. His faith was illimitable.

They came into the sodden dip at the foot of the ridge, and the lightning revealed to him the edge of the poplar growth in which O'Connor had seen Marette many weeks ago. The bayou trail wound through this, and Kent struck out for it blindly in the darkness. He did not try to talk, but he freed his companion's hand and put his arm about her when they came to the level ground, so that she was sheltered by him from the beat of the storm. Then brush swished in their faces, and they stopped, waiting for the lightning again. Kent was not anxious for it to come. He drew the girl still closer, and in that pit of blackness, with the deluge about her and the crash of thunder over her head, she snuggled up against his breast, the throb of her body against him, waiting, watching, with him. Her frailty, the helplessness of her, the slimness of her in the crook of his arm, filled him with an exquisite exultation. He did not think of her now as the splendid, fearless creature who had leveled her little black gun at the three men in barracks. She was no longer the mysterious, defiant, unafraid person who had held him in a sort of awe that first hour in Kedsty's place. For she was crumpled against him now, utterly dependent and afraid. In that chaos of storm something told him that her nerve was broken, that without him she would be lost and would cry out in fear. *And he was glad!* He held her tighter; he bent his head until his face touched the wet, crushed hair under the edge of her turban. And then the lightning split open the night again, and he saw the way ahead of him to the trail.

Even in darkness it was not difficult to follow in the clean-cut wagon path. Over their heads the tops of the poplars swished and wailed. Under their feet the roadway in places was a running stream or inundated until it became a pool. In pitch blackness they struck such a pool, and in spite of the handicap of his packs and rifle Kent stopped suddenly, and picked Marette up in his arms, and carried her until they reached high ground. He did not ask permission. And Marette, for a minute or two, lay crumpled up close in his arms, and for a thrilling instant his face touched her rain-wet cheek.

The miracle of their adventure was that neither spoke. To Kent the silence between them had become a thing which he had no desire to break. In that silence, excused and abetted by the tumult of the storm, he felt that a wonderful something was drawing them closer and closer together, and that words might spoil the indescribable magic of the thing that was happening. When he set Marette on her feet again, her hand accidentally fell upon his, and for a moment her fingers closed upon it in a soft pressure that meant more to him than a thousand words of gratitude.

A quarter of a mile beyond the poplar thicket they came to the edge of the spruce and cedar timber, and Soon the thick walls of the forest shut them in, sheltering them from the wind, but the blackness was even more like that of a bottomless pit. Kent had noticed that the thunder and lightning were drifting steadily eastward, and now the occasional flashes of electrical fire scarcely illumined the trail ahead of them. The rain was not beating so fiercely. They could hear the wail of the spruce and cedar tops and the slush of their boots in mud and water. An interval came, where the spruce-tops met overhead, when it was almost calm. It was then that Kent threw out of him a great, deep breath and laughed joyously and exultantly.

"Are you wet, little Gray Goose?"

"Only outside, Big Otter. My feathers have kept me dry."

Her voice had a trembling, half-sobbing, half-rejoicing note in it. It was not the voice of one who had recently killed a man. In it was a pathos which Kent knew she was trying to hide behind brave words. Her hands clung to the arm of his rubber slicker even as they stood there, close together, as if she was afraid something might drag them apart in that treacherous gloom. Kent, fumbling for a moment, drew from an inner pocket a dry handkerchief. Then he found her face, tilted it a bit upward, and wiped it dry. He might have done the same thing to a child who had been crying. After that he scrubbed his own, and they went on, his arm about her again.

It was half a mile from the edge of the forest to the bayou, and half a dozen times in that distance Kent took the girl in his arms and carried her through water that almost reached his boot tops. The lightning no longer served them. The rain still fell steadily, but the wind had gone with the eastward sweep of the storm. Close-hung with the forest walls, the bayou itself was indiscernible in the blackness. Marette guided him now, though Kent walked ahead of her, holding firmly to her hand. Unless Fingers had changed its location, the scow should be somewhere within forty or fifty paces of the end of the trail. It was small, a two-man scow, with a tight little house built amidships. And it was tied close up against the shore. Marette told him this as they felt their way through brush and reeds. Then he stumbled against something taut and knee-high, and he found it was the tie-rope.

Leaving Marette with her back to the anchor tree, he went aboard. The water was three or four inches deep in the bottom of the scow, but the cabin was built on a platform raised above the floor of the boat, and Kent hoped it was still dry. He groped until he found the twisted wire which held the door shut. Opening it, he ducked his head low and entered. The little room was not more than four feet high, and for greater convenience he fell upon his knees while fumbling under his slicker for his water-proof box of matches. The water had not yet risen above the floor.

The first light he struck revealed the interior to him. It was a tiny cabin, scarcely larger than some boxes he had seen. It was about eight feet long by six in width, and the ceiling was so low that, even kneeling, his head touched it. His match burned out, and he lighted another. This time he saw a candle stuck in a bit of split birch that projected from the wall. He crept to it and lighted it. For a moment he looked about him, and again he blessed Fingers. The little scow was prepared for a voyage. Two narrow bunks were built at the far end, one so close above the other that Kent grinned as he thought of squeezing between. There were blankets. Within reach of his arm was a tiny stove, and close to the stove a supply of kindling and dry wood. The whole thing made him think of a child's playhouse. Yet there was still room for a wide, comfortable, cane-bottomed chair, a stool, and a smooth-planed board fastened under a window, so that it answered the purpose of a table. This table was piled with many packages.

He stripped off his packs and returned for Marette. She had come to the edge of the scow and called to him softly as she heard him splashing through the water. Her arms were reaching toward him, to meet him in the darkness. He carried her through the shallow sea about his feet and laughed as he put her down on the edge of the platform at the door. It was a low, joyous laugh. The yellow light of the candle sputtered in their wet faces. Only dimly could he see her, but her eyes were shining.

"Your nest, little Gray Goose," he cried gently.

Her hand reached up and touched his face. "You have been good to me, Jeems," she said, a little tremble in her voice. "You may—kiss me."

Out in the beat of the rain Kent's heart choked him with song. His soul swelled with the desire to shout forth a paean of joy and triumph at the world he was leaving this night for all time. With the warm thrill of Marette's lips he had become the superman, and as he leaped ashore in the darkness and cut the tie-rope with a single slash of his knife, he wanted to give voice to the thing that was in him as the rivermen had chanted in the glory of their freedom the day the big brigade started north. And he *did* sing, under his laughing, sobbing breath. With a giant's strength he sent the scow out into the bayou, and then back and forth he swung the long one-man sweep, twisting the craft riverward with the force of two pairs of arms instead of one. Behind the closed door of the tiny cabin was all that the world now held worth fighting for. By turning his head he could see the faint illumination of the candle at the window. The light—the cabin—Marette!

He laughed inanely, foolishly, like a boy. He began to hear a dull, droning murmur, a sound that with each stroke of the sweep grew into a more distinct, cataract-like roar. It was the river. Swollen by flood, it was a terrifying sound. But Kent did not dread it. It was *his* river; it was his friend. It was the pulse and throb of life to him now. The growing tumult of it was not menace, but the joyous thunder of many voices calling to him, rejoicing at his coming. It grew in his ears. Over his head the black sky opened again, and a deluge of rain fell straight down. But above the sound of it the rush of the river drew nearer, and still nearer. He felt the first eddying swirl of it against the scow head, and powerful hands seemed to reach in out of the darkness. He knew that the nose of the current had caught him and was carrying him out on the breast of the stream. He shipped the sweep and straightened himself, facing the utter chaos of blackness ahead. He felt under him the slow and mighty pulse of the great flood as it swept toward the Slave, the Mackenzie, and the Arctic. And he cried out at last in the downpour of storm, a cry of joy, of exultation, of hope that reached beyond the laws of men—and then he turned toward the little cabin, where through the thickness of sodden night the tiny window was glowing yellow with candle-light.

CHAPTER XIX

To the cabin Kent groped his way, and knocked, and it was Marette who opened the door for him and stepped back for him to enter. Like a great wet dog he came in, doubling until his hands almost touched the floor. He sensed the incongruity of it, the misplacement of his overgrown body in this playhouse thing, and he grinned through the trickles of wet that ran down his face, and tried to see. Marette had taken off her turban and rain-coat, and she, too, stooped low in the four-feet space of the cabin—but not so ridiculously low as Kent. He dropped on his knees again. And then he saw that in the tiny stove a fire was burning. The crackle of it rose above the beat of the rain on the roof, and the air was already mellowing with the warmth of it. He looked at Marette. Her wet hair was still clinging to her face, her feet and arms and part of her body were wet; but her eyes were shining, and she was smiling at him. She seemed to him, in this moment, like a child that was glad it had found refuge. He had thought that the terror of the night would show in her face, but it was gone. She was not thinking of the thunder and the lightning, the black trail, or of Kedsty lying dead in his bungalow. She was thinking of him.

He laughed outright. It was a joyous, thrilling thing, this black night with the storm over their heads and the roll of the great river under them—they two—alone—in this cockleshell cabin that was not high enough to stand in and scarcely big enough in any direction to turn round in. The snug cheer of it, the warmth of the fire beginning to reach their chilled bodies, and the inspiring crackle of the birch in the little stove filled Kent, for a space, with other thoughts than those of the world they were leaving. And Marette, whose eyes and lips were smiling at him softly in the candle-glow, seemed also to have forgotten. It was the little window that brought them back to the tragedy of their flight. Kent visioned it as it must look from the shore— a telltale blotch of light traveling through the darkness. There were occasional cabins for several miles below the Landing, and eyes turned riverward in the storm might see it. He made his way to the window and fastened his slicker over it.

"We're off, Gray Goose," he said then, rubbing his hands. "Would it seem more homelike if I smoked?"

She nodded, her eyes on the slicker at the window.

"It's pretty safe," said Kent, fishing out his pipe, and beginning to fill it. "Everybody asleep, probably. But we won't take any chances." The scow was swinging sideways in the current. Kent felt the change in its movement, and added: "No danger of being wrecked, either. There isn't a rock or rapids for thirty miles. River clear as a floor. If we bump ashore, don't get frightened."

"I'm not afraid—of the river," she said. Then, with rather startling unexpectedness, she asked him, "Where will they look for us tomorrow?"

Kent lighted his pipe, eyeing her a bit speculatively as she seated herself on the stool, leaning toward him as she waited for an answer to her question.

"The woods, the river, everywhere," he said. "They'll look for a missing boat, of course. We've simply got to watch behind us and take advantage of a good start."

"Will the rain wipe out our footprints, Jeems?"

"Yes. Everything in the open."

"But—perhaps—in a sheltered place—?"

"We were in no sheltered place," he assured her. "Can you remember that we were, Gray Goose?"

She shook her head slowly. "No. But there was Mooie, under the window."

"His footprints will be wiped out."

"I am glad. I would not have him, or M'sieu Fingers, or any of our friends brought into this trouble."

She made no effort to hide the relief his words brought her. He was a little amazed that she should worry over Fingers and the old Indian in this hour of their own peril. That danger he had decided to keep as far from her mind as possible. But she could not help realizing the impending menace of it. She must know that within a few hours Kedsty would be found, and the long arm of the wilderness police would begin its work. And if it caught them—

She had thrust her feet toward him and was wriggling them inside her boots, so that he heard the slushing sound of water. "Ugh, but they are wet!" she shivered. "Will you unlace them and pull them off for me, Jeems?"

He laid his pipe aside and knelt close to her. It took him five minutes to get the boots off. Then he held one of her sodden little feet close between his two big hands.

"Cold—cold as ice," he said. "You must take off your stockings, Marette. Please."

He arranged a pile of wood in front of the stove and covered it with a blanket which he pulled from one of the bunks. Then, still on his knees, he drew the cane chair close to the fire and covered it with a second blanket. A few moments later Marette was tucked comfortably in this chair, with her bare feet on the blanketed pile of wood. Kent opened the stove door. Then he extinguished one of the smoking candles, and after that, the other. The flaming birch illumined the little cabin with a mellower light. It gave a subdued flush to the girl's face. Her eyes seemed to Kent wonderfully soft and beautiful in that changed light. And when he had finished, she reached out a hand, and for an instant it touched his face and his wet hair so lightly that he sensed the thrilling caress of it without feeling its weight.

"You are so good to me, Jeems," she said, and he thought there was a little choking note in her throat.

He had seated himself on the floor, close to her chair, with his back to the wall. "It is because I love you, Gray Goose," he replied quietly, looking straight into the fire.

She was silent. She, too, was looking into the fire. Close over their heads they heard the beating of the rain, like a thousand soft little fists pounding the top of the cabin. Under them they could feel the slow swinging of the scow as it responded to the twists and vagaries of the current that was carrying them on. And Kent, unseen by the girl who was looking away from him, raised his eyes. The birch light was glowing in her hair; it trembled on her white throat; her long lashes were caught in the shimmer of it. And, looking at her, Kent thought of Kedsty lying back in his bungalow room, choked to death by a tress of that glorious hair, so near to him now that, by leaning a little forward, he might have touched it with his lips. The thought brought him no horror. For even as he looked, one of her hands crept up to her cheek—the small, soft hand that had touched his face and hair as lightly as a bit of thistle-down—and he knew that two hands like that could not have killed a man who was fighting for life when he died.

And Kent reached up, and took the hand, and held it close in his own, as he said, "Little Gray Goose, please tell me now—what happened in Kedsty's room?"

His voice thrilled with an immeasurable faith. He wanted her to know, no matter what had happened, that this faith and his love for her could not be shaken. He believed in her, and would always believe in her.

Already he was sure that he knew how Kedsty had died. The picture of the tragedy had pieced itself together in his mind, bit by bit. While he slept, Marette and a man were down in the big room with the Inspector of Police. The climax had come, and Kedsty was struck a blow—in some unaccountable way—with his own gun. Then, just as Kedsty was recovering sufficiently from the shock of the blow to fight, Marette's companion had killed him. Horrified, dazed by what had already happened, perhaps unconscious, she had been powerless to prevent the use of a tress of her hair in the murderer's final work. Kent, in this picture, eliminated the boot-laces and the curtain cords. He knew that the unusual and the least expected happened frequently in crime. And Marette's long hair was flowing loose about her. To use it had simply been the first inspiration of the murderer. And Kent believed, as he waited for her answer now, that Marette would tell him this.

And as he waited, he felt her fingers tighten in his hand.

"Tell me, Gray Goose—what happened?"

"I—don't—know—Jeems—"

His eyes went to her suddenly from the fire, as if he was not quite sure he had heard what she had said. She did not move her head, but continued to gaze unseeingly into the flames. Inside his palm her fingers worked to his thumb and held it tightly again, as they had clung to it when she was frightened by the thunder and lightning.

"I don't know what happened, Jeems."

This time he did not feel the clinging thrill of her little fingers and soft palm. Deep within him he experienced something that was like a sudden and unexpected blow. He was ready to fight for her until his last breath was gone. He was ready to believe anything she told him—anything except this impossible thing which she had just spoken. For she did know what had happened in Kedsty's room. She knew—unless—

Suddenly his heart leaped with joyous hope. "You mean—you were unconscious?" he cried in a low voice that trembled with his eagerness. "You fainted—and it happened then?"

She shook her head. "No. I was asleep in my room. I didn't intend to sleep, but—I did. Something awakened me. I thought I had been dreaming. But something kept pulling me, pulling me downstairs. And when I went, I found Kedsty like that. He was dead. I was paralyzed, standing there, when you came."

She drew her, hand away from him, gently, but significantly. "I know you can't believe me, Jeems. It is impossible for you to believe me."

"And you don't want me to believe you, Marette."

"Yes—I do. You must believe me."

"But the tress of hair—your hair—round Kedsty's neck—"

He stopped. His words, spoken gently as they were, seemed brutal to him. Yet he could not see that they affected her. She did not flinch. He saw no tremor of horror. Steadily she continued to look into the fire. And his brain grew confused. Never in all his experience had he seen such absolute and unaffected self-control. And somehow, it chilled him. It chilled him even as he wanted to reach out and gather her close in his arms, and pour his love into her ears, entreating her to tell him everything, to keep nothing back from him that might help in the fight he was going to make.

And then she said, "Jeems, if we should be caught by the Police—it would probably be quite soon, wouldn't it?"

"They won't catch us."

"But our greatest danger of being caught is right now, isn't it?" she insisted.

Kent took out his watch and leaned over to look at it in the fireglow. "It is three o'clock," he said. "Give me another day and night, Gray Goose, and the Police will never find us."

For a moment or two more she was silent. Then her hand reached out, and her fingers twined softly round his thumb again. "Jeems—when we are safe—when we are sure the Police won't find us—I will tell you all that I know—about what happened in Kedsty's room. And I will tell you— about—the hair. I will tell you—everything." Her fingers tightened almost fiercely. "Everything," she repeated. "I will tell you about that in Kedsty's room—and I will tell you about myself—and after that—I am afraid—you won't like me."

"I love you," he said, making no movement to touch her. "No matter what you tell me, Gray Goose, I shall love you."

She gave a little cry, scarcely more than a broken note in her throat, and Kent—had her face been turned toward him then—would have seen the glory that came into it, and into her eyes, like a swift flash of light—and passed as swiftly away.

What he did see, when she turned her head, were eyes caught suddenly by something at the cabin door. He looked. Water was trickling in slowly over the sill.

"I expected that," he said cheerfully. "Our scow is turning into a rain-barrel, Marette. Unless I bail out, we'll soon be flooded."

He reached for his slicker and put it on. "It won't take me long to throw the water overboard," he added. "And while I'm doing that I want you to take *off* your wet things and tuck yourself into bed. Will you, Gray Goose?"

"I'm not tired, but if you think it is best—" Her hand touched his arm.

"It is best," he said, and for a moment he bent over her until his lips touched her hair.

Then he seized a pail, and went out into the rain.

CHAPTER XX

It was that hour when, with clear skies, the gray northern dawn would have been breaking faintly over the eastern forests. Kent found the darkness more fog-like; about him was a grayer, ghostlier sort of gloom. But he could not see the water under his feet. Nor could he see the rail of the scow, or the river. From the stern, ten feet from the cabin door, the cabin itself was swallowed up and invisible.

With the steady, swinging motion of the riverman he began bailing. So regular became his movements that they ran in a sort of rhythmic accompaniment to his thoughts. The monotonous *splash, splash, splash* of the outflung pails of water assumed, after a few minutes, the character of a mechanical thing. He could smell the nearness of the shore. Even in the rain the tang of cedar and balsam came to him faintly.

But it was the river that impressed itself most upon his senses. It seemed to him, as the minutes passed, like a living thing. He could hear it gurgling and playing under the end of the scow. And with that sound there was another and more indescribable thing, the tremble of it, the pulse of it, the thrill of it in the impenetrable gloom, the life of it as it swept on in a slow and mighty flood between its wilderness walls. Kent had always said, "You can hear the river's heart beat—if you know how to listen for it." And he heard it now. He felt it. The rain could not beat it out, nor could the splash of the water he was throwing overboard drown it, and the darkness could not hide it from the vision that was burning like a living coal within him. Always it was the river that had given him consolation in times of loneliness. For him it had grown into a thing with a soul, a thing that personified hope, courage, comradeship, everything that was big and great in final achievement. And tonight—for he still thought of the darkness as night—the soul of it seemed whispering to him a sort of paean.

He could not lose. That was the thought that filled him. Never had his pulse beat with greater assurance, never had a more positive sense of the inevitable possessed him. It was inconceivable, he thought, even to fear the possibility of being taken by the Police. He was more than a man fighting for his freedom alone, more than an individual struggling for the right to exist. A thing vastly more priceless than either freedom or life, if they were to be accepted alone, waited for him in the little cabin, shut in by its sea of darkness. And ahead of them lay their world. He emphasized that. *Their* world—the world which, in an illusive and unreal sort of way, had been a part of his dreams all his life. In that world they would shut themselves in. No one would ever find them. And the glory of the sun and the stars and God's open country would be with them always.

Marette was the very heart of that reality which impinged itself upon him now. He did not worry about what it was she would tell him tomorrow, or day after tomorrow. He believed that it was then—when she had told him what there was to tell, and he still reached, out his arms to her—that she would come into those arms. And he knew that nothing that might have happened in Kedsty's room would keep his arms from reaching, to her. Such was his faith, potent as the mighty flood hidden in the gray-ghost gloom of approaching dawn.

Yet he did not expect to win easily. As he worked, his mind swept up and down the Three Rivers from the Landing to Fort Simpson, and mentally he pictured the situations that might arise, and how he would triumph over them. He figured that the men at Barracks would not enter Kedsty's bungalow until noon at the earliest. The Police gasoline launch would probably set out on a river search soon after. By mid-afternoon the scow would have a fifty-mile start.

Before darkness came again they would be through the Death Chute, where Follette and Ladouceur swam their mad race for the love of a girl. And not many miles below the Chute was a swampy country where he could hide the scow. Then they would start overland, west and north. Given until another sunset, and they would be safe. This was what he expected. But if it came to fighting—he would fight.

The rain had slackened to a thin drizzle by the time he finished his bailing. The aroma of cedar and balsam came to him more clearly, and he heard more distinctly the murmuring surge of the river. He tapped again at the door of the cabin, and Marette answered him.

The fire had burned down to a bed of glowing coals when he entered. Again he fell on his knees, and took off his dripping slicker.

The girl greeted him from the berth. "You look like a great bear, Jeems." There was a glad, welcoming note in her voice.

He laughed, and drew the stool beside her, and managed to sit on it, the roof compelling him to bend his head over a little. "I feel like an elephant in a birdcage," he replied. "Are you comfortable, little Gray Goose?"

"Yes. But you, Jeems? You are wet!"

"But so happy that I don't feel it, Gray Goose."

He could make her out only dimly there in the darkness of the berth. Her face was a pale shadow, and she had loosened her damp hair so that the warmth and dry air might reach it more easily. Kent wondered if she could hear the beating of his heart. He forgot the fire, and the darkness grew thicker. He could no longer see the pale outline of her face, and he drew back a little, possessed by the thought that it was sacrilegious to bend nearer to her, like a thief, in that gloom. She sensed his movement, and her hand reached to him and lay lightly with its fingertips touching his arm.

"Jeems," she said softly. "I'm not sorry—now—that I came up to Cardigan's place that day—when you thought you were dying. I wasn't wrong. You are different. And I made fun of you then, and laughed at you, because I knew that you were not going to die. Will you forgive me?"

He laughed happily. "It's funny how little things work out, sometimes," he said. "Wasn't a kingdom lost once upon a time because some fellow didn't have a horseshoe? Anyway, I knew of a man whose life was saved because of a broken pipe-stem. And you came to me, and I'm here with you now, because—"

"Of what?" she whispered.

"Because of something that happened a long time ago," he said. "Something you wouldn't dream could have anything to do with you or with me. Shall I tell you about it, Marette?"

Her fingers pressed slightly upon his arm. "Yes."

"Of course, it's a story of the Police," he began. "And I won't mention this fellow's name. You may think of him as that red-headed O'Connor, if you want to. But I don't say that it was he. He was a constable in the Service and had been away North looking up some Indians who were brewing an intoxicating liquor from roots. That was six years ago. And he caught something. Le Mort Rouge, we sometimes call it—the Red Death—or smallpox. And he was alone when the fever knocked him down, three hundred miles from anywhere. His Indian ran away at the first sign of it, and he had just time to get up his tent before he was flat on his back. I won't try to tell you of the days he went through. It was a living death. And he would have died, there is no doubt of it, if it hadn't been for a stranger who came along. He was a white man. Marette, it doesn't take a great deal of nerve to go up against a man with a gun, when you've got a gun of your own; and it doesn't take such a lot of nerve to go into battle when a thousand others are going with you. But it does take nerve to face what that stranger faced. And the sick man was nothing to him. He went into that tent and nursed the other back to life. Then the sickness got him, and for ten weeks those two were together, each fighting to save the other's life, and they won out. But the glory of it was with the stranger. He was going west. The constable was going south. They shook hands and parted."

Marette's fingers tightened on Kent's arm. And Kent went on.

"And the constable never forgot, Gray Goose. He wanted the day to come when he might repay. And the time came. It was years later, and it worked out in a curious way. A man was murdered. And the constable, who had become a sergeant now, had talked with the dead man only a little while before he was killed. Returning for something he had forgotten, it was the sergeant who found him dead. Very shortly afterward a man was arrested. There was blood on his clothing. The evidence was convincing, deadly. And this man—"

Kent paused, and in the darkness Marette's hand crept down his arm to his hand, and her fingers closed round it.

"Was the man you lied to save," she whispered.

"Yes. When the halfbreed's bullet got me, I thought it was a good chance to repay Sandy McTrigger for what he did for me in that tent years before. But it wasn't heroic. It wasn't even brave. I thought I was going to die and that I was risking nothing."

And then there came a soft, joyous little laugh from where her head lay on the pillow. "And all the time you were lying so splendidly, Jeems—I KNEW," she cried. "I knew that you didn't kill Barkley, and I knew that you weren't going to die, and I knew what happened in that tent ten years ago. And—Jeems—Jeems—"

She raised herself from the pillow. Her breath was coming a little excitedly. Both her hands, instead of one, were gripping his hand now. "I knew that you didn't kill John Barkley," she repeated. "And—*Sandy McTrigger didn't kill him!*"

"But—"

"He *didn't*," she interrupted him, almost fiercely. "He was innocent, as innocent as you were. Jeems—I Jeems—I know who killed Barkley. Oh, I *know—I know!*"

A choking sob came into her throat, and then she added, in a voice which she was straining to make calm, "Don't think that I haven't faith in you because I can't tell you more now, Jeems," she said. "You will understand— quite soon. When we are safe from the Police, I shall tell you. I shall keep nothing from you then. I shall tell you about Barkley, and Kedsty— everything. But I can't now. It won't be long. When you tell me we are safe, I shall believe you. And then—" She withdrew her hands from his and dropped back on her pillow.

"And then—what?" he asked, leaning far over.

"You may not like me, Jeems."

"I love you," he whispered. "Nothing in the world can stop my loving you."

"Even if I tell you—soon—that I killed Barkley?"

"No. You would be lying."

"Or—if I told you—that I—killed—Kedsty?"

"No matter what you said, or what proof there might be back there, I would not believe you."

She was silent. And then, "Jeems—"

"Yes, Niska, Little Goddess—?"

"I'm going to tell you something—now!"

He waited.

"It is going to—shock you—Jeems."

He felt her arms reaching up. Her two hands touched his shoulders.

"Are you listening?"

"Yes, I am listening."

"Because I'm not going to say it very loud." And then she whispered, "Jeems—*I love you*!"

CHAPTER XXI

In the slowly breaking gloom of the cabin, with Marette's arms round his neck, her soft lips given him to kiss, Kent for many minutes was conscious of nothing but the thrill of his one great hope on earth come true. What he had prayed for was no longer a prayer, and what he had dreamed of was no longer a dream; yet for a space the reality of it seemed unreal. What he said in those first moments of his exaltation he would probably never remember.

His own physical existence seemed a thing trivial and almost lost, a thing submerged and swallowed up by the warm beat and throb of that other life, a thousand times more precious than his own, which he held in his arms. Yet with the mad thrill that possessed him, in the embrace of his arms, there was an infinite tenderness, a gentleness, that drew from Marette's lips a low, glad whispering of his name. She drew his head down and kissed him, and Kent fell upon his knees at her side and crushed his face close down to her—while outside the patter of rain on the roof had ceased, and the fog-like darkness was breaking with gray dawn.

In that dawn of the new day Kent came at last out of the cabin and looked upon a splendid world. In his breast was the glory of a thing new-born, and the world, like himself, was changed. Storm had passed. The gray river lay under his eyes. Shoreward he made out the dark outlines of the deep spruce and cedar and balsam forests. About him there was a great stillness, broken only by the murmur of the river and the ripple of water under the scow. Wind had gone with the black rainclouds, and Kent, as he looked about him, saw the swift dissolution of the last shadows of night, and the breaking in the East of a new paradise. In the East, as the minutes passed, there came a soft and luminous gray, and after that, swiftly, with the miracle of far Northern dawn, a vast, low-burning fire seemed to start far beyond the forests, tinting the sky with a delicate pink that crept higher and higher as Kent watched it. The river, all at once, came out of its last drifting haze of fog and night. The scow was about in the middle of the channel. Two hundred yards on either side were thick green walls of forest glistening fresh and cool with the wet of storm and breathing forth the perfume which Kent was drawing deep into his lungs.

In the cabin he heard sound. Marette was up, and he was eager to have her come out and stand with him in this glory of their first day. He watched the smoke of the fire he had built, hardwood smoke that drifted up white and clean into the rain-washed air.

The smell of it, like the smell of balsam and cedar, was to Kent the aroma of life. And then he began to clean out what was left of the water in the bottom of the scow, and as he worked he whistled. He wanted Marette to hear that whistle. He wanted her to know that day had brought with it no doubt for him. A great and glorious world was about them and ahead of them. And they were safe.

As he worked, his mind became more than ever set upon the resolution to take no chances. He paused in his whistling for a moment to laugh softly and exultantly as he thought of the years of experience which were his surest safeguard now. He had become almost uncannily expert in all the finesse and trickery of his craft of hunting human game, and he knew what the man-hunters would do and what they would not do. He had them checkmated at the start. And, besides—with Kedsty, O'Connor, and himself gone—the Landing was short-handed just at present. There was an enormous satisfaction in that. But even with a score of men behind him Kent knew that he would beat them. His hazard, if there was peril at all, lay in this first day. Only the Police gasoline launch could possibly overtake them. And with the start they had, he was sure they would pass the Death Chute, conceal the scow, and take to the untracked forests north and west before the launch could menace them. After that he would keep always west and north, deeper and deeper into that wild and untraveled country which would be the last place in which the Law would seek for them. He straightened himself and looked at the smoke again, drifting like gray-white lace between him and the blue of the sky, and in that moment the sun capped the tall green tops of the highest cedars, and day broke gloriously over the earth.

For a quarter of an hour longer Kent mopped at the floor of the scow, and then—with a suddenness that drew him up as if a whip-lash had snapped behind him—he caught another aroma in the clean, forest-scented air. It was bacon and coffee! He had believed that Marette was taking her time in putting on dry footwear and making some sort of morning toilet. Instead of that, she was getting breakfast. It was not an extraordinary thing to do. To fry bacon and make coffee was not, in any sense, a remarkable achievement. But at the present moment it was the crowning touch to Kent's paradise. She was getting HIS breakfast! And—coffee and bacon—To Kent those two things had always stood for home. They were intimate and companionable. Where there were coffee and bacon, he had known children who laughed, women who sang, and men with happy, welcoming faces. They were home-builders.

"Whenever you smell coffee and bacon at a cabin," O'Connor had always said, "they'll ask you in to breakfast if you knock at the door."

But Kent was not recalling his old trail mate's words. In the present moment all other thoughts were lost in the discovery that Marette was getting breakfast—for him.

He went to the door and listened. Then he opened it and looked in. Marette was on her knees before the open door of the stove, toasting bread on two forks. Her face was flushed pink. She had not taken time to brush her hair, but had woven it carelessly into a thick braid that fell down her back. She gave a little exclamation of mock disappointment when she saw Kent.

"Why didn't you wait?" she remonstrated. "I wanted to surprise you."

"You have," he said. "And I couldn't wait. I had to come in and help."

He was inside the door and on his knees beside her. As he reached for the two forks, his lips pressed against her hair. The pink deepened in Marette's face, and the soft little note that was like laughter came into her throat. Her hand caressed his cheek as she rose to her feet, and Kent laughed back. And after that, as she arranged things on the shelf table, her hand now and then touched his shoulder, or his hair, and two or three times he heard that wonderful little throat-note that sent through him a wild pulse of happiness. And then, he sitting in the low chair and she on the stool, they drew close together before the board that answered as a table, and ate their breakfast. Marette poured his coffee and stirred sugar and condensed milk in it, and so happy was Kent that he did not tell her he used neither milk nor sugar in his coffee. The morning sun burst through the little window, and through the open door Kent pointed to the glory of it on the river and in the shimmering green of the forests slipping away behind. When they had finished, Marette went outside with him.

For a space she stood silent and without movement, looking upon the marvelous world that encompassed them. It seemed to Kent that for a few moments she did not breathe. With her head thrown back and her white throat bare to the soft, balsam-laden air she faced the forests. Her eyes became suddenly filled with the luminous glow of stars. Her face reflected the radiance of the rising sun, and Kent, looking at her, knew that he had never seen her so beautiful as in these wonderful moments. He held his own breath, for he also knew that Niska, his goddess, was looking upon her own world again after a long time away.

Her world—and his. Different from all the other worlds God had ever made; different, even, from the world only a few miles behind them at the Landing. For here was no sound or whisper of destroying human life. They were in the embrace of the Great North, and it was drawing them closer, and with each minute nearer to the mighty, pulsing heart of it.

The forests hung heavy and green and glistening with the wet of storm; out of them came the tremulous breath of life and the glory of living; they hugged the shores like watchful hosts guarding the river from civilization—and suddenly the girl held out her arms, and Kent heard the low, thrilling cry that came to her lips.

She had forgotten him. She had forgotten everything but the river, the forests, and the untrod worlds beyond them, and he was glad. For this world that she was welcoming, that her soul was crying out to, was his world, for ever and ever. It held his dreams, his hopes, all the desires that he had in life. And when at last Marette turned toward him slowly, his arms were reaching out to her, and in his face she saw that same glory which filled her own.

"I'm glad—glad," she cried softly. "Oh, Jeems—I'm glad!"

She came into his arms without hesitation; her hands stroked his face; and then she stood with her head against his shoulder, looking ahead, breathing deeply now of the sweet, clear air filled with the elixir of the hovering forests. She did not speak, or move, and Kent remained quiet. The scow drifted around a bend. Shoreward a great moose splashed up out of the water, and they could hear him afterward, crashing through the forest. Her body tensed, but she did not speak. After a little he heard her whisper,

"It has been a long time, Jeems. I have been away four years."

"And now we are going home, little Gray Goose. You will not be lonely?"

"No. I was lonely down there. There were so many people, and so many things, that I was homesick for the woods and mountains. I believe I would have died soon. There were only two things I loved, Jeems—"

"What?" he asked.

"Pretty dresses—and shoes."

His arms closed about her a little more tightly. "I—I understand," he laughed softly. "That is why you came, that first time, with pretty high-heeled pumps."

He bowed his head, and she turned her face to him. On her upturned mouth he kissed her.

"More than any other man ever loved a woman I love you, Niska, little goddess," he cried.

The minutes and the hours of that day stood out ever afterward in Kent's life as unforgettable memories. There were times when they seemed illusory and unreal, as though he lived and breathed in an insubstantial world made up of gossamer things which must be the fabric of dream. These were moments when the black shadow of the tragedy from which they were fleeing pressed upon him, when the thought came to him that they were criminals racing with the law; that they were not on enchanted ground, but in deadly peril; that it was all a fools' paradise from which some terrible shock would shortly awaken him. But these periods of apprehension were, in themselves, mere shadows thrown for a moment upon his happiness. Again and again the subconscious force within him pounded home to his physical brain the great truth, that it was all extraordinarily real.

It was Marette who made him doubt himself at times. He could not, quite yet, comprehend the fulness of that love which she had given him. More than ever, in the glory of this love that had come to them she was like a child to him. It seemed to him in the first hours of the morning that she had forgotten yesterday, and the day before, and all the days before that. She was going home. She whispered that to him so often that it became a little song in his brain. Yet she told him nothing of that home, and he waited, knowing that the fulfilment of her promise was not far away. And there was no embarrassment in the manner of her surrender when he held her in his arms, and she held her face up, so that he could kiss her mouth and look into her glowing, lovely eyes. What he saw was the flush of a great happiness, the almost childish confession of it along with the woman's joy of possession. And he thought of Kedsty, and of the Law that was rousing itself into life back at Athabasca Landing.

And then she ran her fingers through his own and told him to wait, and ran into the cabin and came out a moment later with her brush; and after that she seated herself at the fulcrum of the big sweep and began to brush out her hair in the sun.

"I'm glad you love it, Jeems," she said.

She unbound the thick braid and let the silken strands of it run caressingly between her fingers. She smoothed it out, brushed it until it was more beautiful than he had ever seen it, in that glow of the sun. She held it up so that it rippled out in shimmering cascades about her—and then, suddenly, Kent saw the short tress from which had been clipped the rope of hair that he had taken from Kedsty's neck. And as his lips tightened, crushing fiercely the exclamation of his horror, there came a trembling happiness from Marette's lips, scarcely more than the whisper of a song, the low, thrilling melody of *Le Chaudière*.

Her arms reached up, and she drew his head down to her, so that for a time his visions were blinded in that sweet smother of her hair.

The intimacy of that day was in itself like a dream. Hour after hour they drifted deeper into the great North. The sun shone. The forest-walled shores of the river grew mightier in their stillness and their grandeur, and the vast silence of unpeopled places brooded over the world. To Kent it was as if they were drifting through Paradise. Occasionally he found it necessary to work the big sweep, for still water was gradually giving way to a swifter current.

Beyond that there was no labor for him to perform. It seemed to him that with each of these wonderful hours danger was being left farther and still farther behind them. Watching the shores, looking ahead, listening for sound that might come from behind—at times possessed of the exquisite thrills of children in their happiness—Kent and Marette found the gulf of strangeness passing swiftly away from between them.

They did not speak of Kedsty, or the tragedy, or again of the death of John Barkley. But Kent told of his days in the North, of his aloneness, of the wild, weird love in his soul for the deepest wildernesses. And from that he went away back into dim and distant yesterdays, alive with mellowed memories of boyhood days spent on a farm. To all these things Marette listened with glowing eyes, with low laughter, or with breath that rose or fell with his own emotions.

She told of her own days down at school and of their appalling loneliness; of childhood spent in the forests; of the desire to live there always. But she did not speak intimately of herself or her life in its more vital aspects; she said nothing of the home in the Valley of Silent Men, nothing of father or mother, sisters or brothers. There was no embarrassment in her omissions. And Kent did not question. He knew that those were among the things she would tell him when that promised hour came, the hour when he would tell her they were safe.

There began to possess him now a growing eagerness for this hour, when they should leave the river and take to the forests. He explained to Marette why they could not float on indefinitely. The river was the one great artery through which ran the blood of all traffic to the far North. It was patrolled. Sooner or later they would be discovered. In the forests, with a thousand untrod trails to choose, they would be safe. He had only one reason for keeping to the river until they passed through the Death Chute. It would carry them beyond a great swampy region to the westward through which it would be impossible for them to make their way at this season of the year. Otherwise he would have gone ashore now. He loved the river, had faith in it, but he knew that not until the deep forests swallowed them, as a vast ocean swallows a ship, would they be beyond the peril that threatened them from the Landing.

Three or four times between sunrise and noon they saw life ashore and on the stream; once a scow tied to a tree, then an Indian camp, and twice trappers' shacks built in the edge of little clearings. With the beginning of afternoon Kent felt growing within him something that was not altogether eagerness. It was, at times, a disturbing emotion, a foreshadowing of evil, a warning for him to be on his guard. He used the sweep more, to help their progress in the current, and he began to measure time and distance with painstaking care. He recognized many landmarks.

By four o'clock, or five at the latest, they would strike the head of the Chute. Ten minutes of its thrilling passage and he would work the scow into the concealment he had in mind ashore, and no longer would he fear the arm of the law that reached out from the Landing. As he planned, he listened. From noon on he never ceased to listen for that distant *putt, putt, putt*, that would give them a mile's warning of the approach of the patrol launch.

He did not keep his plans to himself. Marette sensed his growing uneasiness, and he made her a partner of his thoughts.

"If we hear the patrol before we reach the Chute, we'll still have time to run ashore," he assured her. "And they won't catch us. We'll be harder to find than two needles in a haystack. But it's best to be prepared."

So he brought out his pack and Marette's smaller bundle, and laid his rifle and pistol holster across them.

It was three o'clock when the character of the river began to change, and Kent smiled happily. They were entering upon swifter waters. There were places where the channel narrowed, and they sped through rapids. Only where unbroken straight waters stretched out ahead of them did Kent give his arms a rest at the sweep. And through most of the straight water he added to the speed of the scow. Marette helped him. In him the exquisite thrill of watching her slender, glorious body as it worked with his own never grew old. She laughed at him over the big oar between them. The wind and sun played riot in her hair. Her parted lips were rose-red, her cheeks flushed, her eyes like sun-warmed rock violets. More than once, in the thrill of that afternoon flight, as he looked at the marvelous beauty of her, he asked himself if it could be anything but a dream. And more than once he laughed joyously, and paused in his swinging of the sweep, and proved that it was real and true. And Kent thanked God, and worked harder.

Once, a long time ago, Marette told him, she had been through the Chute. It had horrified her then. She remembered it as a sort of death monster, roaring for its victims. As they drew nearer to it, Kent told her more about it. Only now and then was a life lost there now, he said. At the mouth of the Chute there was a great, knife-like rock, like a dragon's tooth, that cut the Chute into two roaring channels. If a scow kept to the left-hand channel it was safe. There would be a mighty roaring and thundering as it swept on its passage, but that roaring of the Chute, he told her, was like the barking of a harmless dog.

Only when a scow became unmanageable, or hit the Dragon's Tooth, or made the right-hand channel instead of the left, was there tragedy. There was that delightful little note of laughter in Marette's throat when Kent told her that.

"You mean, Jeems, that if one of three possible things doesn't happen, we'll get through safely?"

"None of them is possible—with us," he corrected himself quickly. "We've a tight little scow, we're not going to hit the rock, and we'll make the left-hand channel so smoothly you won't know when it happens." He smiled at her with splendid confidence. "I've been through it a hundred times," he said.

He listened. Then, suddenly, he drew out his watch. It was a quarter of four. Marette's ears caught what he heard. In the air was a low, trembling murmur. It was growing slowly but steadily. He nodded when she looked at him, the question in her eyes.

"The rapids at the head of the Chute!" he cried, his voice vibrant with joy. "We've beat them out. *We're safe*!"

They swung around a bend, and the white spume of the rapids lay half a mile ahead of them. The current began to race with them now. Kent put his whole weight on the sweep to keep the scow in mid-channel.

"We're safe," he repeated. "Do you understand, Marette? _We're safe_!"

He was speaking the words for which she had waited, was telling her that at last the hour had come when she could keep her promise to him. The words, as he gave them voice, thrilled him. He felt like shouting them. And then all at once he saw the change that had come into her face. Her wide, startled eyes were not looking at him, but beyond. She was looking back in the direction from which they had come, and even as he stared her face grew white.

"*Listen*!"

She was tense, rigid. He turned his head. And in that moment it came to him above the growing murmur of the river—the *putt, putt, putt* of the Police patrol boat from Athabasca Landing!

A deep breath came from between his lips. When Marette took her eyes from the river and looked at him, his face was like carven rock. He was staring dead ahead.

"We can't make the Chute," he said, his voice sounding hard and unreal to her. "If we do, they'll be up with us before we can land at the other end. We must let this current drive us ashore—*now*."

As he made his decision, he put the strength of his body into action. He knew there was not the hundredth part of a second to lose. The outreaching suction of the rapids was already gripping the scow, and with mighty strokes he fought to work the head of his craft toward the westward shore. With swift understanding Marette saw the priceless value of a few seconds of time. If they were caught in the stronger swirl of the rapids before the shore was reached, they would be forced to run the Chute, and in that event the launch would be upon them before they could make a landing farther on. She sprang to Kent's side and added her own strength in the working of the sweep. Foot by foot and yard by yard the scow made precious westing, and Kent's face lighted up with triumph as he nodded ahead to a timbered point that thrust itself out like a stubby thumb into the river. Beyond that point the rapids were frothing white, and they could see the first black walls of rock that marked the beginning of the Chute.

"We'll make it," he smiled confidently. "We'll hit that timbered point close inshore. I don't see where the launch can make a landing anywhere within a mile of the Chute. And once ashore we'll make trail about five times as fast they can follow it." Marette's face was no longer pale, but flushed with excitement. He caught the white gleam of teeth between her parted lips. Her eyes shone gloriously, and he laughed.

"You beautiful little fighter," he cried exultantly. "You—you—"

His words were cut short by a snap that was like the report of a pistol close to his ears. He pitched forward and crashed to the bottom of the scow, Marette's slim body clutched in his arms as he fell. In a flash they were up, and mutely they stared where the sweep had been. The blade of it was gone. Kent was conscious of hearing a little cry from the girl at his side, and then her fingers were gripping tightly again about his thumb. No longer possessed of the power of guidance, the scow swung sideways. It swept past the wooded point. The white maelstrom of the lower rapids seized upon it. And Kent, looking ahead to the black maw of the death-trap that was waiting for them, drew Marette close in his arms and held her tight.

CHAPTER XXII

For a brief space after the breaking of the scow-sweep Kent did not move. He felt Marette's arms closing tighter and tighter around his neck. He caught a flash of her upturned face, the flush of a few moments before replaced by a deathly pallor, and he knew that without explanation on his part she understood the almost hopeless situation they were in. He was glad of that. It gave him a sense of relief to know that she would not go into a panic, no matter what happened. He bowed his face to hers, so that he felt the velvety smoothness of her cheek. She turned her mouth to him, and they kissed. His embrace was crushing for a moment, fierce with his love for her, desperate with his determination to keep her from harm.

His brain was working swiftly. There was possibly one chance in ten that the scow—rudderless and without human guidance—would sweep safely between the black walls and jagged teeth of the Chute. Even if the scow made this passage, they would be in the power of the Police, unless some splendid whimsicality of Fate sent it ashore before the launch came through.

On the other hand, if it was carried far enough through the lower rapids, they might swim. And—there was the rifle laying across the pack. That, after all, was his greatest hope—if the scow made the passage of the Chute. The bulwarks of the scow would give them greater protection than the thinner walls of the launch would give to their pursuers. In his heart there raged suddenly a hatred for that Law of which he had been a part. It was running them to destruction, and he would fight. There would not be more than three men in the launch, and he would kill them, if killing became a necessity.

They were speeding like an unbridled race-horse through the boiling rapids now. The clumsy craft under their feet twisted and turned. The dripping tops of great rocks shot past a little out of their channel. And Marette, with one arm still about his neck, was facing the peril ahead with him. They could see the Dragon's Tooth, black and grim, waiting squarely in their path. In another hundred and twenty seconds they would be upon it—or past it. There was no time for Kent to explain. He sprang to his pack, whipped a knife from his pocket, and cut the stout babiche rope that reenforced its straps. In another instant he was back at Marette's side, fastening the babiche about her waist. The other end he gave to her, and she tied it about his wrist. She smiled as she finished the knot. It was a strange, tense little smile, but it told him that she was not afraid, that she had great faith in him, and knew what the babiche meant.

"I can swim, Jeems," she cried. "If we strike the rock."

She did not finish because of the sudden cry that came to his lips. He had almost forgotten the most vital of all things. There was not time to unlace his boots. With his knife he cut the laces in a single downward thrust. Swiftly he freed his own feet, and Marette's. Even in this hour of their peril it thrilled him to see how quickly Marette responded to the thoughts that moved him. She tore at her outer garments and slipped them off as he wriggled out of his heavy shirt. A slim, white-underskirted little thing, her glorious hair flying in the wind that came through the Chute, her throat and arms bare, her eyes shining at Kent, she came again close within his arms, and her lips framed softly his name. And a moment later she turned her face up, and cried quickly,

"Kiss me, Jeems—kiss me—"

Her warm lips clung to his, and her bare arms encircled his neck with the choking grip of a child's. He looked ahead and braced himself on his feet, and after that he buried one of his hands in the soft mass of her hair and pressed her face against his naked breast.

Ten seconds later the crash came. Squarely amidships the scow struck the Dragon's Tooth. Kent was prepared for the shock, but his attempt to hold his feet, with Marette in his arms, was futile. The bulwark saved them from crashing against the slippery face of the rock itself. Amid the roar of water that filled his ears he was conscious of the rending of timbers. The scow bulged up with the mighty force beneath, and for a second or two it seemed as though that force was going to overturn and submerge it. Then slowly it began to slip off the nose of the rock.

Holding to the rail with one hand and clinging to Marette with his other arm, Kent was gripped in the horror of what was happening. The scow was slipping *into the right hand channel!* In that channel there was no hope—only death.

Marette was squarely facing the thing ahead. In this hour when each second held a lifetime of suspense Kent saw that she understood. Yet she did not cry out. Her face was dead white. Her hair and arms and shoulders were dripping with the splash of water. But she was not terrified as he had seen terror. When she turned her eyes to him, he was amazed by the quiet, calm look that was in them. Her lips trembled.

His soul expressed itself in a wordless cry that was drowned in another crash of timber as a jutting snag of the Tooth crumpled up the little cabin as if it had been pasteboard. He felt overwhelming him the surge of a thing mightier than the menace of the Chute. He could not lose! It was inconceivable. Impossible! With *her* to fight for—this slim, wonderful creature who smiled at him even as she saw death.

And then, as his arm closed still more tightly about her, the monsters of power and death gave him their answer. The scow swung free of the Dragon's Tooth, half-filled with water. Its cracked and broken carcass was caught in the rock jaws of the eastern channel. It ceased to be a floating thing. It was inundation, dissolution, utter obliteration almost without shock. And Kent found himself in the thundering rush of waters, holding to Marette.

For a space they were under. Black water and white froth fumed and exploded over them. It seemed an age before fresh air filled Kent's nostrils. He thrust Marette upward and cried out to her. He heard her answer.

"I'm all right—Jeems!"

His swimming prowess was of little avail now. He was like a chip. All his effort was to make of himself a barrier between Marette's soft body and the rocks. It was not the water itself that he feared, but the rocks.

There were scores and hundreds of them, like the teeth of a mighty grinding machine. And the jaw was a quarter of a mile in length. He felt the first shock, the second, the third. He was not thinking of time or distance, but was fighting solely to keep himself between Marette and death. The first time he failed, a blind sort of rage burned in his brain.

He saw her white body strained over a slippery, deluge-worn rock. Her head was flung back, and he saw the long masses of her hair streaming out in the white froth, and he thought for an instant that her fragile body had been broken. He fought still more fiercely after that. And she knew for what he was fighting. Only in an unreal sort of way was he conscious of shock and hurt. It gave him no physical pain. Yet he sensed the growing dizziness in his head, an increasing lack of strength in his arms and body.

They were halfway through the Chute when he shot against a rock with terrific force. The contact tore Marette from him. He plunged for her, missed his grip, and then saw her opposite him, clinging to the same rock. The babiche rope had saved her. Fastened about her waist and tied to his wrist, it still held them together—with the five feet of rock between them.

Panting, their life half beaten out of them, their eyes met over that rock. Now that he was out of the water, the blood began streaming from Kent's arms and shoulders and face, but he smiled at her as a few moments before she had smiled at him. Her eyes were filled with the pain of his hurts. He nodded back in the direction from which they had come.

"We're out of the worst of it," he tried to shout. "As soon as we've got our wind, I will climb over the rock to you. It won't take us longer than a couple of minutes, perhaps less, to make the quiet water at the end of the channel."

She heard him and nodded her reply. He wanted to give her confidence. And he had no intention of resting, for her position filled him with a terror which he fought to hide. The babiche rope, not half as large around as his little finger, had swung her to the downstream side of the rock. It was the slender thread of buckskin and his own weight that were holding her. If the buckskin should break—

He thanked God that it was the tough babiche that had been around his pack. An inch at a time he began to draw himself up on the rock. The undertow behind the rock had flung a mass of Marette's long hair toward him, so that it was a foot or two nearer to him than her clinging hands. He worked himself toward that, for he saw that he could reach it more quickly than he could reach her. At the same time he had to keep his end of the babiche taut. It was, from the beginning, an almost superhuman task. The rock was slippery as oil. Twice his eyes shot down-stream, with the thought that it might be better to cast himself bodily into the water, and after that draw Marette to him by means of the babiche. What he saw convinced him that such action would be fatal. He must have Marette in his arms. If he lost her—even for a few seconds—the life would be beaten from her body in that rock-strewn maelstrom below.

And then, suddenly, the babiche cord about his wrist grew loose. The reaction almost threw him back. With the loosening of it a cry came from Marette. It all happened in an instant, in almost less time than his brain could seize upon the significance of it—the slipping of her hands from the rock, the shooting of her white body away from him in the still whiter spume of the rapids, The rock had cut the babiche, and she was gone! With a cry that was like the cry of a madman he plunged after her. The water engulfed him. He twisted himself up, freeing himself from the undertow. Twenty feet ahead of him—thirty—he caught a glimpse of a white arm and then of Marette's face, before she disappeared in a wall of froth.

Into that froth he shot after her. He came out of it blinded, groping wildly for her, crying out her name. His fingers caught the end of the babiche that was fastened about his own wrist, and he clutched it savagely, believing for a moment that he had found her. Thicker and more deadly the rocks of the lower passage rose in his way. They seemed like living things, like devils filled with the desire to torture and destroy. They struck and beat at him. Their laughter was the roar of a Niagara. He no longer cried out. His brain grew heavy, and clubs were beating him—beating and breaking him into a formless thing. The rock-drifts of spume, lather-white, like the frosting of a monster cake, turned gray and then black.

He did not know when he ceased fighting. The day went out. Night came. The world was oblivion. And for a space he ceased to live.

CHAPTER XXIII

An hour later the fighting forces in his body dragged Kent back into existence. He opened his eyes. The shock of what had happened did not at once fall upon him. His first sensation was of awakening from a sleep that had been filled with pain and horror.

Then he saw a black rock wall opposite him; he heard the sullen roar of the stream; his eyes fell upon a vivid patch of light reflected from the setting sun. He dragged himself up until he was on his knees, and all at once a thing that was like an iron hoop—choking his senses—seemed to break in his head, and he staggered to his feet, crying out Marette's name. Understanding inundated him with its horror, deadening his tongue after that first cry, filling his throat with a moaning, sobbing agony. Marette was gone. She was lost. She was dead.

Swiftly, as reason came, his eyes took in his environment. For a quarter of a mile above him he could see the white spume between the chasm walls, darkening with the approach of night. He could hear more clearly the roar of the death-floods. But close to him was smooth water, and he stood now on a shelving tongue of rock and shale, upon which the current had flung him. In front of him was a rock wall. Behind him was another. There was no footing except where he stood. And Marette was not with him.

Only the truth could batter at his brain as he stood there. But his physical self refused to accept that truth. If he had lived, she must live! She was there—somewhere—along the shore—among the rocks—

The moaning in his throat gave way to the voicing of her name. He shouted, and listened. He swayed back along the tongue of rock to the boulder-strewn edge of the chasm wall. A hundred yards farther on was the opening of the Chute. He came out of this, his clothes torn from him, his body bleeding, unrecognizable, half a madman,—shouting her name more and more loudly. The glow of the setting sun struck him at last. He was out from between the chasm walls, and it lighted up the green world for him. Ahead of him the river widened and swept on in tranquil quiet.

And now it was no longer fear that possessed him. It was the horrible, overwhelming certainty of the thing. The years fell from him, and he sobbed—sobbed like a boy stricken by some great childish grief, as he searched along the edge of the shore. Over and over again he cried and whispered Marette's name.

But he did not shout it again, for he knew that she was dead. She was gone from him forever. Yet he did not cease to search. The last of the sun went out. Twilight came, and then darkness. Even in that darkness he continued to search for a mile below the Chute, calling her name more loudly now, and listening always for the answer which he knew would never come. The moon came out after a time, and hour after hour he kept up his hopeless quest. He did not know how badly the rocks had battered and hurt him, and he scarcely knew when it was that exhaustion dropped him like a dead man in his tracks. When dawn came, it found him wandering away from the river, and toward noon of that day, he was found by André Boileau, the old white-haired half-breed who trapped on Burntwood Creek. André was shocked at the sight of his wounds and half dragged and half carried him to his shack hidden away in the forest.

For six days thereafter Kent remained at old André's place, simply because he had neither the strength nor the reason to move. André wondered that there were no broken bones in him. But his head was terribly hurt, and it was that hurt that for three days and three nights made Kent hover with nerve-racking indecision between life and death. The fourth day reason came back to him, and Boileau fed him venison broth. The fifth day he stood up. The sixth he thanked André, and said that he was ready to go.

André outfitted him with old clothes, gave him a supply of food and God's blessing. And Kent returned to the Chute, giving André to understand that his destination was Athabasca Landing.

Kent knew that it was not wise for him to return to the river. He knew that it would have been better for him both in mind and body had he gone in the opposite direction. But he no longer had in him the desire to fight, even for himself. He followed the lines of least resistance, and these led him back to the scene of the tragedy. His grief, when he returned, was no longer the heartbreaking agony of that first night. It was a deep-seated, consuming fire that had already burned him out, heart and soul. Even caution was dead in him. He feared nothing, avoided nothing. Had the police boat been at the Chute, he would have revealed himself without any thought of self-preservation. A ray of hope would have been precious medicine to him. But there was no hope. Marette was dead. Her tender body was destroyed. And he was alone, unfathomably and hopelessly alone.

And now, after he had reached the river again, something held him there. From the head of the Chute to a bend in the river two miles below, his feet wore a beaten trail. Three or four times a day he would make the trip, and along the path he set a few snares in which he caught rabbits for food. Each night he made his bed in a crevice among the rocks at the foot of the Chute. At the end of a week the old Jim Kent was dead. Even O'Connor would not have recognized him with his shaggy growth of beard, his hollow eyes, and the sunken cheeks which the beard failed to hide.

And the fighting spirit in him also was dead. Once or twice there leaped up in him a sudden passion demanding vengeance upon the accursed Law that was accountable for the death of Marette, but even this flame snuffed itself out quickly.

And then, on the eighth day, he saw the edge of a thing that was almost hidden under an overhanging bank. He fished it out. It was Marette's little pack, and for many minutes before he opened it Kent crushed the sodden treasure to his breast, staring with half-mad eyes down where he had found it, as if Marette must be there, too. Then he ran with it to an open space, where the sun fell warmly on a great, flat rock that was level with the ground, and with sobbing breath he opened it. It was filled with the things she had picked up quickly in her room the night of their flight from Kedsty's bungalow, and as he drew them out one by one and placed them in the sun on the rock, a new and sudden rush of life swept through his veins, and he sprang to his feet and faced the river again, as if at last a hope had come to him. Then he looked down again upon what she had treasured, and reaching out his arms to them, he whispered,

"Marette—my little goddess—"

Even in his grief the overwhelming mastery of his love for the one who was dead brought a smile to his haggard and bearded face. For Marette, in filling her little pack on that night of hurried flight, had chosen strange things. On the sunlit rock, where he had placed them, were a pair of the little pumps which he had fallen on his knees to worship in her room, and with these she had crowded into the pack one of the billowing, sweet-smelling dresses which had made his heart stand still for a moment when he first looked into their hiding-place. It was no longer soft and cobwebby as it had been then, like down fluttering against his cheeks, but sodden and discolored, as it lay on the rock with little rivulets of water running from it.

With the shoes and the dress were the intimate necessities which Marette had taken with her. But it was one of the pumps that Kent picked up and crushed close to his ragged breast—one of the two she had worn that first wonderful day she had come to see him at Cardigan's place.

This hour was the beginning of another change in Kent. It seemed to him that a message had come to him from Marette herself, that the spirit of her had returned to him and was with him now, stirring strange things in his soul and warming his blood with a new heat. She was gone forever, and yet she had come back to him, and the truth grew upon him that this spirit of her would never leave him again as long as he lived. He felt her nearness. Unconsciously he reached out his arms, and a strange happiness entered Into him to battle with grief and loneliness. His eyes shone with a new glow as they looked at her little belongings on the sunlit rock. It was as if they were flesh and blood of her, a part of her heart and soul. They were the voice of her faith in him, her promise that she would be with him always. For the first time in many days Kent felt a new force within him, and he knew that she was not quite gone, that he had something of her left to fight for.

That night he made his bed for a last time in the crevice between the rocks, and his treasure was gathered within the protecting circle of his arms as he slept.

The next day he struck out north and east. On the fifth day after he left the country of André Boileau he traded his watch to a half-breed for a cheap gun, ammunition, a blanket, flour, and a cooking outfit. After that he had no hesitation in burying himself still deeper into the forests.

A month later no one would have recognized Kent as the one-time crack man of N Division. Bearded, ragged, long-haired, he wandered with no other purpose than to be alone and to get still farther away from the river. Occasionally he talked with an Indian or a half-breed. Each night, though the weather was very warm, he made himself a small camp-fire, for it was always in these hours, with the fire-light about him, that he felt Marette was very near. It was then that he took out one by one the precious things that were in Marette's little pack. He worshipped these things. The dress and each of the little shoes he had wrapped in the velvety inner bark of the birch tree. He protected them from wet and storm. Had emergency called for it, he would have fought for them. They became, after a time, more precious than his own life, and in a vague sort of way at first he began to thank God that the river had not robbed him of everything.

Kent's inclination was not to fight himself into forgetfulness. He wanted to remember every act, every word, every treasured caress that chained him for all time to the love he had lost. Marette became more a part of him every day. Dead in the flesh, she was always at his side, nestling close in the shelter of his arms at night, walking with her hand in his during the day. And in this belief his grief was softened by the sweet and merciful comfort of a possession of which neither man nor fate could rob him—a beloved Presence always with him.

It was this Presence that rebuilt Kent. It urged him to throw up his head again, to square his shoulders, to look life once more straight in the face. It was both inspiration and courage to him and grew nearer and dearer to him as time passed. Early Autumn found him in the Fond du Lac country, two hundred miles east of Fort Chippewyan. That Winter he joined a Frenchman, and until February they trapped along the edges of the lower fingers of the Barrens.

He came to think a great deal of Picard, his comrade. But he revealed nothing of his secret to him, or of the new desire that was growing in him. And as the Winter lengthened this desire became a deep and abiding yearning. It was with him night and day. He dreamed of it when he slept, and it was never out of his thoughts when awake. He wanted to go HOME. And when he thought of home, it was not of the Landing, and not of the country south. For him home meant only one place in the world now—the place where Marette had lived. Somewhere, hidden in the mountains far north and west, was that mysterious Valley of Silent Men where they had been going when her body died. And the spirit of her wanted him to go to it now. It was like a voice pleading with him, urging him to go, to live there always where she had lived. He began to plan, and in this planning he found new joy and new life. He would find her home, her people, the valley that was to have been their paradise. So late in February, with his share of the Winter catch in his pack, he said good-by to Picard and faced the River again.

CHAPTER XXIV

Kent had not forgotten that he was an outlaw, but he was not afraid. Now that he had something new and thrilling to fight for, he fell back again upon what he called "the finesse of the game." He approached Chippewyan cautiously, although he was sure that even his old friends at the Landing would fail to recognize him now. His beard was four or five inches long, and his hair was shaggy and uncut. Picard had made him a coat, that winter, of young caribou skin, and it was fringed like an Indian's. Kent chose his time and entered Chippewyan just before dusk.

Oil lamps were burning in the Hudson's Bay Company's store when he went in with his furs. The place was empty, except for the factor's clerk, and for an hour he bartered. He bought a new outfit, a Winchester rifle, and all the supplies he could carry. He did not forget a razor and a pair of shears, and when he was done he still had the value of two silver fox skins in cash. He left Chippewyan that same night, and by the light of a Winter moon made his camp half a dozen miles northward toward Smith Landing.

He was on the Slave River now and for weeks traveled slowly but steadily northward on snowshoes. He avoided Fort Smith and Smith Landing and struck westward before he came to Fort Resolution. It was in April that he struck Hay River Post, where the Hay River empties into Great Slave Lake. Until the ice broke up, Kent worked at Hay River. When it was safe, he started down the Mackenzie in a canoe. It was late in June when he turned up the Liard to the South Nahani.

"You go straight through between the sources of the North and the South Nahani," Marette had told him. "It is there you find the Sulphur Country, and beyond the Sulphur Country is the Valley of Silent Men."

At last he came to the edge of this country. He camped with the stink of it in his nostrils. The moon rose, and he saw that desolate world as through the fumes of a yellow smoke. With dawn he went on.

He passed through broad, low morasses out of which rose sulphurous fogs. Mile after mile he buried himself deeper in it, and it became more and more a dead country, a lost hell. There were berry bushes on which there grew no berries. There were forests and swamps, but without a living creature to inhabit them.

It was a country of water in which there were no fish, of air in which there were no birds, of plants without flowers—a reeking, stinking country still with the stillness of death. He began to turn yellow. His clothing, his canoe, his hands, face—everything turned yellow. He could not get the filthy taste of sulphur out of his mouth. Yet he kept on, straight west by the compass

Gowen had given him at Hay River. Even this compass became yellow in his pocket. It was impossible for him to eat. Only twice that day did he drink from his flask of water.

And Marette had made this journey! He kept telling himself that. It was the secret way in and out of their hidden world, a region accursed by devils, a forbidden country to both Indian and white man. It was hard for him to believe that she had come this way, that she had drunk in the air that was filling his own lungs, nauseating him a dozen times to the point of sickness. He worked desperately. He felt neither fatigue nor the heat of the warm water about him.

Night came, and the moon rose, lighting up with a sickly glow the diseased world that had swallowed him. He lay in the bottom of his canoe, covering his face with his caribou coat, and tried to sleep. But sleep would not come. Before dawn he struck on, watching his compass by the light of matches. All that day he made no effort to swallow food. But with the coming of the second night he found the air easier to breathe. He fought his way on by the light of the moon which was clearer now. And at last, in a resting spell, he heard far ahead of him the howl of a wolf.

In his joy he cried out. A western breeze brought him air that he drank in as a desert-stricken man drinks water. He did not look at his compass again, but worked steadily in the face of that fresh air. An hour later he found that he was paddling again a slow current, and when he tasted the water it was only slightly tainted with sulphur. By midnight the water was cool and clean. He landed on a shore of sand and pebbles, stripped to the skin, and gave himself such a scouring as he had never before experienced. He had worn his old trapping shirt and trousers, and after his bath he changed to the outfit which he had kept clean in his pack. Then he built a fire and ate his first meal in two days.

The next morning he climbed a tall spruce and surveyed the country about him. Westward there was a broad low country shut in fifteen or twenty miles away by the foothills. Beyond these foothills rose the snow-capped peaks of the Rockies. He shaved himself, cut his hair, and went on. That night he camped only when he could drive his canoe no farther. The waterway had narrowed to a creek, and he was among the first green shoulders of the hills when he stopped. With another dawn he concealed his canoe in a sheltered place and went on with his pack.

For a week he picked his way slowly westward. It was a splendid country into which he had come, and yet he found no sign of human life. The foothills changed to mountains, and he believed he was in the Campbell Range. Also he knew that he had followed the logical trail from the sulphur country. Yet it was the eighth day before he came upon a sign which told him that another living being had at some time passed that way. What he found were the charred remnants of an old camp-fire. It had been a white man's fire. He knew that by the size of it. It had been an all-night fire of green logs cut with an axe.

On the tenth day he came to the westward slope of the first range and looked down upon one of the most wonderful valleys his eyes had ever beheld. It was more than a valley. It was a broad plain. Fifty miles across it rose the towering majesty of the mightiest of all the Yukon mountains.

And now, though he saw a paradise about him, his heart began to sink within him. It seemed to him inconceivable that in a country so vast he could find the spot for which he was seeking. His one hope lay in finding white men or Indians, some one who might guide him.

He traveled slowly over the fifty-mile plain rich with a verdure of green, covered with flowers, a game paradise. Few hunters had come so far out of the Yukon mountains, he told himself. And none had come from out of the sulphur country. It was a new and undiscovered world. On his map it was a blank space. And there were no signs of people. Ahead of him the Yukon mountains rose in an impenetrable wall, peak after peak, crested with snow, towering like mighty watchdogs above the clouds. He knew what lay beyond them—the great rivers of the Western slope, Dawson City, the gold country and its civilization. But those things were on the other side of the mountains. On his side there was only the vast and undisputed silence of a paradise as yet unclaimed by man.

As he went on into this valley there grew upon him a strange and comforting peace. Yet with it there was a steadily increasing belief that he would not find that for which he had come in search. He did not attempt to analyze this belief. It became a part of him, just as his mental tranquillity had grown upon him. His one hope of success was that nearer the mountains he might find white men or Indians.

He no longer used his compass, but guided himself by a cluster of three gigantic peaks. One of these was taller than the other two. As he journeyed, his eyes were always returning to it. It fascinated him, impinged itself upon him as the watcher of a million years, guarding the valley. He began to think of it as the Watcher. Each hour of his progress seemed to bring it a little more intimately to his vision. From his first night's camp in the valley he saw the moon sink behind it. Within him a voice that never died kept whispering to him that this mountain, greater than all the others, had been Marette's guardian. Ten thousand times she must have looked at it, as he had looked at it that day—if her home was anywhere this side of the Campbell Range. A hundred miles away she could have seen the Watcher on a clear day.

On the second day the mountain continued to grow upon Kent. By mid-afternoon it began to take on a new character. The peak of it was in the form of a mighty castle that changed as he advanced. And the two lesser peaks were forming into definite contours. Before the haze of twilight dimmed his vision, he knew that what he had seen was not a whimsical invention of his imagination. The Watcher had grown into the shape of a mighty human head facing south. A restless excitement possessed him, and he traveled on long after dusk. At dawn he was on the trail again. Westward the sky cleared, and suddenly he stopped, and a cry came from him.

The Watcher's head was there, as if chiseled by the hands of giants. The two smaller peaks had unveiled their mystery. Startling and weird, their crests had taken on the form of human heads. One of them was looking north. The other faced the valley. And Kent, his heart pounding, cried to himself,

"The Silent Men!"

He did not hear himself, but the thought itself was a tumultuous thing within him. It came upon him like an inundation, a sudden and thrilling inspiration backed by the forces of a visual truth. *The Valley of Silent Men.* He repeated the words, staring at the three colossal heads in the sky. Somewhere near them, under them,—one side or the other—was Marette's hidden valley!

He went on. A strange joy consumed him. In it, at times, his grief was obliterated, and it seemed to him in these moments that Marette must surely be at the valley to greet him when he came to it. But always the tragedy of the Death Chute came back to him, and with it the thought that the three giant heads were watching—and would always watch—for a beloved lost one who would never return. As the sun went down that day, the face bowed to the valley seemed alive with the fire of a living question sent directly to Kent.

"Where is she?" it asked. "Where is she? Where is she?"

That night Kent did not sleep.

The next day there lay ahead of him a low and broken range, the first of the deeper mountains. He climbed this steadily, and at noon had reached the crest. And he knew that at last he was looking down into the Valley of Silent Men. It was not a wide valley, like the other. On the far side of it, three or four miles away, rose the huge mountain whose face was looking down upon the green meadows at its foot. Southward Kent could see for a long distance, and in the vivid sunlight he saw the shimmer of creeks and little lakes, and the rich glow of thick patches of cedar and spruce and balsam, scattered like great rugs of velvety luster amid the flowering green of the valley. Northward, three or four miles away the range which he had climbed made a sharp twist to the east, and that part of the valley—following the swing of the range— was lost to him. He turned in this direction after he had rested. It was four o'clock when he came to the elbow in the valley, and could look down into the hidden part of it.

What he saw at first was a giant cup hollowed out of the surrounding mountains, a cup two miles from brim to brim, the end of the valley itself. It took him a few moments to focus his vision so that it would pick up the smaller and more intimate things half a mile under him, and yet, before he had done this, a sound came up to him that set aquiver every nerve in his body. It was the far-down, hollow-sounding barking of a dog.

The warm, golden haze that precedes sunset in the mountains, was gathering between him and the valley, but through this he made out after a time evidences of human habitation almost straight under him. There was a small lake out of which ran a shimmering creek, and close to this lake, yet equally near to the base of the mountain on which he was standing, were a number of buildings and a stockade which looked like a toy. He could see no animals, no movement of any kind.

Without seeking for a downward trail he began to descend. Again he did not question himself. An overwhelming certainty possessed him. Of all places in the world this must be the Valley of Silent Men.

And below him, flooded and half-hidden in the illusive sun-mist, was Marette's old home. It seemed to him now that it belonged to him, that he was a part of it, that in going to it he was achieving his last great resting place, his final refuge, his own home. And the thought became strangely a part of him that a welcome must be waiting for him there. He hurried until his breath came pantingly between his lips and he was forced to rest. And at last he found himself where his progress was made a foot at a time, and again and again he was forced to climb back and detour around treacherous slides and precipitous breaks which left sheer falls at his feet. The mist thickened in the valley. The sun sank behind the western peaks, and swiftly after that the gloom of twilight deepened. It was seven o'clock when he came to the edge of the plain, at least a mile below the elbow which shut out the cup in the valley. He was exhausted. His hands were bruised and bleeding. Darkness shut him in when he went on.

When he rounded the elbow of the mountain, he did not try to keep back the joyous cry that came to his lips. Ahead of him there were lights. A few of them were scattered, but nearest to him he saw a cluster of them, like the glow that comes from a number of illumined windows. He quickened his pace as he drew nearer to them, and at last he wanted to run. And then something stopped him, and it seemed to him that his heart had risen into his throat and was choking him until he could not breathe.

It was a man's voice he heard, calling through the twilight gloom a name. "Marette—Marette—Marette—"

Kent tried to cry out, but his breath came only in a gasp. He felt himself trembling. He reached out his arms, and a strange madness rushed like fire into his brain.

Again the voice called, "Marette—Marette—Marette—"

The cup in the valley echoed the name. It rolled softly up the mountainside. The air trembled with it, whispered it, passed it on—and suddenly the madness in Kent found voice, and he shouted,

"Marette—Marette—"

He ran on. His knees felt weak. He shouted the name again, and the other voice was silent. Things loomed up out of the mist ahead of him, between him and the glowing windows. Some one—two people—were advancing to meet him, doubtfully, wonderingly. Kent was staggering, but he cried the name again, and this time it was a woman's cry that answered, and one of the two came toward him swift as a flash of light.

Three paces apart they stood, and in that gloom of the after-twilight their burning eyes looked at each other, while for a space their bodies remained stricken in the face of this miracle of a great and merciful God.

The dead had risen. By a mighty effort Kent reached out his arms, and Marette swayed to him. When the other man came up, he found them crumpled to their knees on the earth, clasped like children in each other's arms. And as Kent raised his face, he saw that it was Sandy McTrigger who was looking down at him, the man whose life he had saved at Athabasca Landing.

CHAPTER XXV

How long it was before his brain cleared, Kent never could have told. It might have been a minute or an hour. Every vital force that was in him had concentrated into a single consciousness—that the dead had come to life, that it was Marette Radisson, the flesh and blood and living warmth of her, he held in his arms. Like the flash of a picture on a screen he had seen McTrigger's face close to him, and then his own head was crushed down again, and if the valley had been filled with the roar of cannon, he would have heard only one sound, a sobbing voice crying over and over again, "Jeems—Jeems—Jeems—"

It was McTrigger, in the beginning of the starlight, who alone looked with clear vision upon the wonder of the thing that was happening. After a little Kent realized that McTrigger was talking, that a hand was on his shoulder, that the voice was both joyous and insistent. He rose to his feet, still holding Marette, her arms clinging to him. Her breath was sobbing and broken. And it was impossible for Kent to speak. He seemed to stumble over the distance between them and the lights, with McTrigger on the other side of Marette. It was McTrigger who opened a door, and they came into a glow of lamplight. It was a great, strange-looking room they entered. And over the threshold Marette's hands dropped from Kent, and Kent stepped back, so that in the light they faced each other, and in that moment came the marvelous readjustment from shock and disbelief to a glorious certainty.

Again Kent's brain was as clear as the day he faced death at the head of the Chute. And swift as a hot barb a fear leaped into him as his eyes met the eyes of the girl. She was terribly changed. Her face was white with a whiteness that startled him. It was thin. Her eyes were great, slumbering pools of violet, almost black in the lamp glow, and her hair—piled high on her head as he had seen it that first day at Cardigan's—added to the telltale pallor in her cheeks. A hand trembled at her throat, and its thinness frightened him. For a space—a flash of seconds—she looked at him as if possessed of the subconscious fear that he was not Jim Kent, and then slowly her arms opened, and she reached them out to him. She did not smile, she did not cry out, she did not speak his name now; but her arms went round his neck as he took her to him, and her face dropped on his breast. He looked at McTrigger. A woman was standing beside him, a dark-haired, dark-eyed woman, and she had laid a hand on McTrigger's arm, Kent, looking at them, understood.

The woman came to him. "I had better take her now, m'sieu," she said. "Malcolm—will tell you. And a little later,—you may see her again."

Her voice was low and soft. At the sound of it Marette raised her head, and her two hands stole to Kent's cheeks in their old sweet way, and she whispered,

"Kiss me, Jeems—my Jeems—kiss me—"

CHAPTER XXVI

A little later, clasping hands in the lamp glow, Kent and Sandy McTrigger stood alone in the big room. In their handclasp was the warm thrill of strong men met in an immutable brotherhood. Each had faced death for the other. Yet this thought, subconsciously and forever a part of them, expressed itself only in the grip of their fingers and in the understanding that lay deep in their eyes.

In Kent's face the great question was of Marette. McTrigger saw the fear of it, and slowly he smiled, a glad and yet an anxious smile, as he looked toward the door through which Marette and the older woman had gone.

"Thank God you have come in time!" he said, still holding Kent's hand. "She thought you were dead. And I know, Kent, that it was killing her. We had to watch her at night. Sometimes she would wander out into the valley. She said she was looking for you. It was that way tonight."

Kent gulped hard. "I understand now," he said. "It was the living soul of her that was pulling me here. I—"

He took his pack with its precious contents from his shoulders, listening to McTrigger. They sat down. What McTrigger was saying seemed of trifling consequence beside the fact that Marette was somewhere beyond the other door, alive, and that he would see her again very soon. He did not see why McTrigger should tell him that the older woman was his wife. Even the fact that a splendid chance had thrown Marette upon a log wedged between two rocks in the Chute, and that this log, breaking away, had carried her to the opposite side of the river miles below, was trivial with the thought that only a door separated them now. But he listened. He heard McTrigger tell how Marette had searched for him those days when he was lost in fever at André Boileau's cabin, how she had given him up for dead, and how in those same days Laselle's brigade had floated down, and she had come north with it. Later he would marvel over these things, but now he listened, and his eyes turned toward the door. It was then that McTrigger drove something home. It was like a shot piercing Kent's brain. McTrigger was speaking quietly of O'Connor. He said:

"But you probably came by way of Fort Simpson, Kent, and O'Connor has told you all this. It was he who brought Marette back home through the Sulphur Country."

"O'Connor!"

Kent sprang to his feet. It took McTrigger but a moment to read the truth in his face.

"Good God, do you mean to tell me you don't know, Kent?" he whispered tensely, rising in front of the other. "Haven't you seen O'Connor? Haven't you come in touch with the Police anywhere within the last year? Don't you know—?"

"I know nothing," breathed Kent.

For a space McTrigger stared at him in amazement

"I have been in hiding," said Kent. "All this time I have been keeping away from the Police."

McTrigger drew a deep breath. Again his hands gripped Kent's, and his voice was incredulous, filled with a great wonder. "And you have come to her, to her old home, believing that Marette killed Kedsty! It is hard to believe. And yet—" Into his face came suddenly a look of grief, almost of pain, and Kent, following his eyes, saw that he was looking at a big stone fireplace in the end of the room.

"It was O'Connor who worked the thing out last Winter," he said, speaking with, an effort. "I must tell you before you see her again. You must understand everything. It will not do to have her tell you. See—"

Kent followed him to the fireplace. From the shelf over the stonework McTrigger took a picture and gave it to him. It was a snapshot, the picture of a bare-headed man standing in the open with the sun shining on him.

A low cry broke from Kent's lips. It was the great, gray ghost of a man he had seen in the lightning flare that night from the window of his hiding-place in Kedsty's bungalow.

"My brother," said McTrigger chokingly. "I loved him. For forty years we were comrades. And Marette belonged to us, half and half. It was he—who killed—John Barkley." And then, after a moment in which McTrigger fought to speak steadily, he added, "And it was he—my brother—who also killed Inspector Kedsty."

For a matter of seconds there was a dead silence between them. McTrigger looked into the fireplace instead of at Kent. Then he said:

"He killed those men, but he didn't murder them, Kent. It couldn't be called that. It was justice, single-man justice, without going to law. If it wasn't for Marette, I wouldn't tell you about it—not the horrible part of it. I don't like to bring it up in my memory. ... It happened years ago. I was not married then, but my brother was ten years older than I and had a wife. I think that Marette loves you as Marie loved Donald. And Donald's love was more than that. It was worship. We came into the new mountain country, the three of us, even before the big strikes at Dawson and Bonanza. It was a wild country, a savage country, and there were few women in it, but Marie came with Donald. She was beautiful, with hair and eyes like Marette's. That was the tragedy of it.

"I won't tell you the details. They were terrible. It happened while Donald and I were out on a hunt. Three men—white men—remember that, Kent; WHITE MEN—came out of the North and stopped at the cabin. When we returned, what we found there drove us mad. Marie died in Donald's arms. And leaving her there, alone, we set out after the white-skinned brutes who had destroyed her. Only a blizzard saved them, Kent. Their trail was fresh when the storm came. Had it held off another two hours, I, too, would have killed.

"From that day Donald and I became man-hunters. We traced the back trail of the three fiends and discovered who they were. Two years later Donald found one of the three on the Yukon, and before he killed him he made him verify the names of the other two. It was a long search after that, Kent. It has covered thirty years. Donald grew old faster than I, and I knew, after a time, that he was strangely mad. He would be gone for months at a time, always searching for the two men. Ten years passed, and then, one day, in the deep of Winter, we came on a cabin home that had been stricken with the plague—the smallpox. It was the home of Pierre Radisson and his wife Andrea. Both were dead. But there was a little child still living, almost a babe in arms. We took her, Donald and I. The child was—Marette."

McTrigger had spoken almost in a monotone. He had not raised his eyes from the ash of the fireplace. But now he looked up suddenly at Kent.

"We worshipped her from the beginning," he said, his voice a bit husky. "I hoped that love for her would save Donald. It did, in a way. But it did not cure his madness, his desire for vengeance. We came farther east. We found this marvelous valley, and gold in the mountains, untouched by other men. We built here, and I hoped even more that the glory of this new world we had discovered would help Donald to forget. I married, and my wife loved Marette. We had a child, and then another, and both died. We loved Marette more than ever after that. Anne, my wife, was the daughter of a missioner and capable of educating Marette up to a certain point. You will find this place filled with all kinds of books, and reading, and music. But the time came when we thought we must send Marette to Montreal. It broke her heart. And then—a long time after—"

McTrigger paused a moment, looking into Kent's eyes. "And then—one day Donald came in from Dawson City, terrible in his madness, and told us that he had found his men. One of them was John Barkley, the rich timber man, and the other was Kedsty, Inspector of Police at Athabasca Landing."

Kent made no effort to speak. His amazement, as McTrigger had gone on, was beyond the expression of words. The night held for him a cumulative shock—the discovery that Marette was not dead, but alive, and now the discovery that he, Jim Kent, was no longer a hunted man, and that it was O'Connor, his old comrade, who had run the truth down. With dry lips he simply nodded, urging McTrigger to continue.

"I knew what would happen if Donald went after Barkley and Kedsty," said the older man. "And it was impossible to hold him back. He was mad, clean mad. There was just one thing for me to do. I left here first, with the intention of warning the two brutes who had killed Donald's wife. I knew, with the evidence in our hands, they could do nothing but make a getaway. No matter how rich or powerful they were, our evidence was complete, and through many years we had kept track of the movements of our witnesses. I tried to explain to Donald that we could send them to prison, but there was but one thought in his poor sick mind—to kill. I was younger and beat him south. And after that I made my fatal mistake. I thought I was far enough ahead of him to get down to the line of rail and back before he arrived. You see, I figured his love for Marette would take him to Montreal first, and I had made up my mind to tell her everything so that she might understand the necessity of holding him if he went to her. I wrote everything to her and told her to remain in Montreal. How she did that, you know. She set out for the North as soon as she received my letter."

McTrigger's shoulders hunched lower. "Well, you know what happened, Kent. Donald got ahead of me, after all. I came the day after Barkley was killed. I took it as a kind fate that the day preceding the killing I shot a grouse for my dinner, and as the bird was only wounded when I picked it up, I got blood on the sleeves of my coat. I was arrested. Kedsty, every one, was sure they had the real man. And I kept quiet, except to maintain my innocence. I could say nothing that would turn the law on Donald's trail.

"After that, things happened quickly. You, my friend, made your false confession to save one who had done you a poor service years ago. Almost simultaneously with that, Marette had come. She came quietly, in the night, and went straight to Kedsty. She told him everything, showed him the written evidence, telling him this evidence was in the hands of others and would be used if anything happened to her. Her power over him was complete. As the price of her secrecy she demanded my release, and in that black hour your confession gave Kedsty his opportunity.

"He knew you were lying. He knew it was Donald who had killed Barkley. Yet he was willing to sacrifice you to save himself. And Marette remained in his house, waiting and watching for Donald, while I searched for him on the trails. That is why she secretly lived in Kedsty's house. She knew that Donald would come there sooner or later, if I did not find him and get him away. And she was plotting how to save you.

"She loved you, Kent—from that first hour she came to you in the hospital. And she tried to exact your freedom also as an added price for her secrecy. But Kedsty had become like a cornered tiger. If he freed you, he saw his whole world crumbling under his feet. He, too, went a little mad, I think. He told Marette that he would not free you, that he would go to the hangman first. Then, Kent, came the night of your freedom, and a little later—Donald came to Kedsty's home. It was he whom you saw that night out in the storm. He entered and killed Kedsty.

"Something dragged Marette down to the room that night. She found Kedsty in his chair—dead. Donald was gone. It was then that you found her there. Kent, she loved you—and you will never know how her heart bled when she let you think she had killed Kedsty. She has told me everything. It was her fear for Donald, her desire to keep all possible suspicion from him until he was safe, that compelled her not to confide even in you. Later, when she knew that Donald must be safe, she was going to tell you. And then—you were separated at the Chute." McTrigger paused, and Kent saw him choke back a grief that was still like the fresh cut of a knife in his heart.

"And O'Connor found out all this?"

McTrigger nodded. "Yes. He defied Kedsty's command to go to Fort Simpson and was on his way back to Athabasca Landing when he found my brother. It is strange how all things happened, Kent. But I guess God must have meant it that way. Donald was dying. And in dying, for a space, his old reason returned to him. It was from him, before he died, that O'Connor learned everything. The story is known everywhere now. It is marvelous that you did not hear—"

There came an interruption, the opening of a door. Anne McTrigger stood looking at them where a little time before she had disappeared with Marette. There was a glad smile in her face. Her dark eyes were glowing with a new happiness. First they rested on McTrigger's face, and then on Kent's.

"Marette is much better," she said in her soft voice. "She is waiting to see you, M'sieu Kent. Will you come now?"

Like one in a dream Kent went toward her. He picked up his pack, for with its precious contents it had become to him like his own flesh and blood. And as the woman led the way and Kent followed her, McTrigger did not move from the fireplace. In a little while Anne McTrigger came back into the room. Her beautiful eyes were aglow. She was smiling softly, and putting her arms about the shoulders of the man at the fireplace, she whispered:

"I have looked at the night through the window, Malcolm. I think that the stars are bigger and brighter than they have been in a long time. And the Watcher seems like a living god up in the sky. Come, please."

She took his hand, and Malcolm went with her. Over their heads burned a glory of stars. The wind came gently up the valley, cool with the freshness of the mountain-tops, sweet with the smell of meadow and flowers. And when the woman pointed through the glow, Malcolm McTrigger looked up at the Watcher, and for an instant he fancied that he saw what she had seen—something that was life instead of death, a glow of understanding and of triumph in the mighty face of stone above the lace mists of the clouds. For a long time they walked on, and deep in the heart of the woman a voice cried out again and again that the Watcher knew, and that it was a living joy she saw up there, for up to that unmoving and voiceless god of the mountains she had cried and laughed and sung—and even prayed; and with her Marette had also done these things, until at last the pulse and beat of women's souls had given a spirit to a form of rock.

Back in the chateau which Malcolm McTrigger and his brother Donald had built of logs, in a room whose windows faced the Watcher himself, Marette was unveiling the last of mystery for Jim Kent. And this, too, was her hour of triumph. Her lips were red and warm with the flush brought there by Kent's love.

Her face was like the wild roses he had crushed under his feet all that day. For in this hour the world had come to her, and had prostrated itself at her feet. The sacred contents of the pack were in her lap as she leaned back in the great blanketed and pillowed chair that had been her invalid's nest for many days. But it was an invalid's nest no longer. The floods of life were pounding through her body again, and in that hour when Malcolm McTrigger and his wife were gone, Kent looked upon the miracle of its change. And now Marette gave to him a little packet, and while Kent opened it she raised both hands to her head and unbound her hair so that it fell about her in shining and glorious confusion.

Kent, unwrapping a last bit of tissue-paper, found in his hands a long tress of hair.

"See, Jeems, it has grown fast since I cut it that night."

She leaned a little toward him, parting her hair with slim, white fingers so that he saw again where the hair had been clipped the night of Kedsty's death.

And then she said: "You may keep it always if you want to, Jeems, for I cut it from my head when I left you in the room below, and when you—almost—believed I had killed Kedsty. It was this—"

She gave him another packet, and her lips tightened a little as Kent unwrapped it, and another tress of hair shimmered in the lamp glow.

"That was father Donald's," she whispered.

"It—it was all he had left of Marie, his wife. And that night—when Kedsty died—"

"I understand," cried Kent, stopping her. "He choked Kedsty with it until he was dead. And when I found it around Kedsty's neck—you—you let me think it was yours—to save father Donald!"

She nodded. "Yes, Jeems. If the police had come, they would have thought I was guilty. I planned to let them think so until father Donald was safe. But all the time I had here in my breast this other tress, which would prove that I was innocent—when the time came. And now, Jeems—"

She smiled at him again and reached out her hands. "Oh, I feel so strong! And I want to take you out now—and show you my valley—Jeems—our valley—yours and mine—in the starlight. Not tomorrow, Jeems. But tonight. Now."

A little later the Watcher looked down on them, even as it had looked down on another man and another woman who had preceded them. But the stars were bigger and brighter, and the white cap of snow that rested on the Watcher's head like a crown caught the faint gleam of a far-away light; and after that, slowly and wonderfully, other snow-crested mountain-tops caught that greeting radiance of the moon. But it was the Watcher who stood out like a mighty god among them all, and when they came to the elbow in the plain, Marette drew Kent down beside her on a great flat rock and laughed softly as she held his hand tightly in her lap.

"Always, from a little child, I have sat and played on this rock, with the Watcher looking, like that," she said in a low voice. "I have grown to love him, Jeems. And I have always believed that he was gazing off there, night and day, into the east, watching for something that was coming to me. Now I know. It was you, Jeems. And, Jeems, when I was away—down there in the big city—"

Her fingers gripped his thumb in their old way, and Kent waited.

"It was the Watcher that made me want to come home most of all," she went on, a bit of tremble in her voice. "Oh, I grew lonely for him, and I could see him in my dreams at night, watching, watching, watching, and sometimes even calling me. Jeems, do you see that hump on his left shoulder, like a great epaulet?"

"Yes, I see," said Kent.

"Beyond that, on a straight line from here—hundreds of miles away—are Dawson City, the Yukon, the big gold country, men, women, civilization. Father Malcolm and father Donald have never found but one trail to this side of the mountains, and I have been over it three times—to Dawson. But the Watcher's back is on those things. Sometimes I imagine it was he who built those great ramparts through which few men come. He wants this valley alone. And so do I. Alone—with you, and with my people."

Kent drew her close in his arms. "When you are stronger," he whispered, "we will go over that hidden trail together, past the Watcher, toward Dawson. For it must be that over there—we will find—a missioner—" He paused.

"Please go on, Jeems."

"And you will be—my wife."

"Yes, yes, Jeems—forever and ever. But, Jeems"—her arms crept up about his neck—"very soon it will be the first of August."

"Yes—?"

"And in that month there come through the mountains, each year, a man and a woman to visit us—mother Anne's father and mother. And mother Anne's father—"

"Yes—?"

"Is a missioner, Jeems."

And Kent, looking up in this hour of his triumph and joy, believed that in the Watcher's face he caught for an instant the passing radiance of a smile.

THE END

Milton Keynes UK
Ingram Content Group UK Ltd.
UKHW030741071024
449371UK00006B/672

9 789362 095770